CONTENTS

PART FOUR
CRITICAL HISTORY

PART FIVE
BACKGROUND

YORK NOTES

GREAT EXPECTATIONS

CHARLES DICKENS

NOTES BY NIGEL MESSENGER

 Longman   York Press

The right of Nigel Messenger to be identified as Author
of this Work has been asserted by him in accordance with the
Copyright, Designs and Patents Act 1988

YORK PRESS
322 Old Brompton Road, London SW5 9JH

PEARSON EDUCATION LIMITED
Edinburgh Gate, Harlow,
Essex CM20 2JE, United Kingdom
Associated companies, branches and representatives throughout the world

First published 1998
This new and fully revised edition first published 2003
Seventh impression 2009

ISBN: 978-0-582-78427-7

Designed by Michelle Cannatella
Typeset by Land & Unwin (Data Sciences), Bugbrooke, Northamptonshire
Produced by Pearson Education Asia Limited, Hong Kong

PART ONE

INTRODUCTION

HOW TO STUDY A NOVEL

Studying a novel on your own requires self-discipline and a carefully thought-out work plan in order to be effective.

- You will need to read the novel more than once. Start by reading it quickly for pleasure, then read it slowly and thoroughly.

- On your second reading make detailed notes on the plot, characters and themes of the novel. Further readings will generate new ideas and help you to memorise the details of the story.

- Some of the characters will develop as the plot unfolds. How do your responses towards them change during the course of the novel?

- Think about how the novel is narrated. From whose point of view are events described?

- A novel may or may not present events chronologically: the time-scheme may be a key to its structure and organisation.

- What part do the settings play in the novel?

- Are words, images or incidents repeated so as to give the work a pattern? Do such patterns help you to understand the novel's themes?

- Identify what styles of language are used in the novel.

- What is the effect of the novel's ending? Is the action completed and closed, or left incomplete and open?

- Does the novel present a moral and just world?

- Cite exact sources for all quotations, whether from the text itself or from critical commentaries. Wherever possible find your own examples from the novel to back up your opinions.

- Always express your ideas in your own words.

These York Notes offer an introduction to *Great Expectations* and cannot substitute for close reading of the text and the study of secondary sources.

CONTEXT

Great Expectations was the thirteenth of Dickens' fifteen novels.

READING *GREAT EXPECTATIONS*

Great Expectations is our greatest novel on the perils and cost of upward social mobility. Our society may seem very different from the one that Dickens describes, but the essential problem of retaining personal integrity in a divisive, competitive world remains the same.

Other novelists have always recognised Dickens' consummate craftsmanship exercised under difficult circumstances (for these see **Note on the text**). George Gissing, a fellow Victorian writer, wrote that 'no story in the first person was ever better told', while in more recent times Graham Greene has praised 'the tone of Dickens' secret prose, that sense of a mind speaking to itself with no one there to listen'. Certainly one of the particular pleasures of this Dickens text is the subtle use of first person narrative. There is a constant, dramatic tension between the older, wiser Pip looking back sadly on his childhood pain and, with irony, on the errors of his growing maturity.

The usual pleasures that Dickens provides are here in abundance. This novel has plenty of social comedy, farcical humour, violent melodrama, mystery, narrative excitement and suspense. As well as Pip's moral decline and redemption, Dickens demonstrates his ability to make extreme situations plausible: Magwitch on the marshes or Miss Havisham's morbid decrepitude are rendered with extraordinary poetic power. Dickens has often been criticised for the ramshackle nature of his plots, but here the unlikely coincidences are structurally and morally coherent; they underline the insight that respectable, prosperous society is always implicated in the violent underclass that it excludes. Dickens' social criticism is at its sharpest and most mordant in this text. Pip's denial of his early life, his inevitable moral corruption, the shocking recognition of Magwitch and the rediscovery of his humanity, make this the most classically satisfying as well as the most emotionally moving of all Dickens' stories.

A snob's progress? Critics have always been divided as to Pip's culpability and the true substance of his moral redemption. When

QUESTION

How do the opening scenes on the marshes in *Great Expectations* introduce us to the important themes of the novel?

we come to make our own judgment it will depend on the degree to which we believe any individual is capable of resisting the pressures of a corrupt world. Certainly Pip feels an extraordinary amount of guilt himself. However, when Miss Havisham says 'You made your own snares, *I* never made them' (Chapter 44, p. 360), we may feel she is being somewhat disingenuous. Pip is cruelly treated, misled and exploited by many people. He has a truly horrible childhood; his village is a dreary place with little to recommend it in actuality, although it grows in nostalgic appeal when there is no chance of his returning there to live. Joe Gargery is a wonderful symbol of lost innocence but something of a holy fool: the complexities of modern life seem to defeat him. His instincts may be always right but he lives in an older, simpler world. Do we blame Pip for seeking his wider horizons and wilder dreams elsewhere?

CONTEXT

In its first serial form the early chapters of *Great Expectations* were published in December 1862 so they could be read as another of Dickens' famous Christmas stories. This shows how carefully Dickens considered his first readers and their expectations.

PART TWO

THE TEXT

NOTE ON THE TEXT

Worried about the falling sales of his weekly periodical *All the Year Round*, Dickens began to serialise *Great Expectations* in December 1860.

CHECK THE NET
You can download some of the original weekly instalments on: **http://www.stanford.edu/dept/news/dickens/**

It ran for thirty-six weeks, the final instalment reaching the public in August 1861. Dickens had originally intended to publish his new novel in twenty monthly parts, his favourite form for publishing novels, but financial anxiety drove him to complete one of his finest works in less than a year. However, Dickens still thought of his novel in monthly portions: the manuscript is divided into nine monthly divisions each containing four weekly instalments. The three stages of Pip's expectations fall into three parts (one stage per part), ready for publication in the three volume format that was the common practice at the time. The original weekly instalments were as follows: Part 1: Chapters 1–2; 3–4; 5; 6–7; 8; 9–10; 11; 12–13; 14–15; 16–17; 18; 19. Part 2: 20–1; 22; 23–4; 25–6; 27–8; 29; 30–1; 32–3; 34–5; 36–7; 38; 39. Part 3: 40; 41–2; 43–4; 45–6; 47–8; 49–50; 51–2; 53; 54; 55–6; 57; 58–9.

There was originally no Chapter 59. Dickens had the older Pip return from abroad to see Joe and Biddy but not to return to Satis House. Instead he was to meet Estella, now remarried to a country doctor, briefly in a London street. Bulwer-Lytton, a friend of Dickens and a novelist himself, persuaded Dickens to alter the end to the one we have now. His original readers would know nothing of the change. Its existence came to light with its publication in John Forster's *Life of Charles Dickens* in 1874. Both endings have been defended and the matter has been a critical issue ever since. See **Narrative techniques: Ambiguously everafter** for further discussion of this.

The first three-volume book edition was published by Chapman and Hall in 1861 and a single-volume edition appeared the following year.

Volume eight of the Oxford Clarendon edition, edited by Margaret Cardwell (1993) is the most authoritative version to date. Students are recommended to use the paperback version of this published in World Classics (1994) with an introduction by Kate Flint or the Penguin Classics edition (2003) edited by David Trotter and Charlotte Mitchell. My page references are from this latter edition. There is also a Norton critical edition (1999) edited by David Rosenberg that includes extensive background information, contexts and critical material.

SYNOPSIS

Young Pip is an orphan living with his shrewish sister and her kindly blacksmith husband Joe Gargery. One Christmas Eve he is surprised by an escaped convict and forced to steal food and a file. The convict is recaptured when he is discovered fighting with another. A year later, Pip is forced to play at Satis House, a gloomy mansion where all time has stopped and everything is decayed. Miss Havisham, a rich spinster, has lived there in seclusion since she was abandoned on her wedding day. He meets a beautiful young girl called Estella whom he adores although she mocks his humble origins. These visits continue until Pip is ready to take up his apprenticeship as a blacksmith. After his visits to Satis House, Pip is discontented with his lot and dreams of becoming a gentleman and marrying Estella. His sister is brutally assaulted with a leg-iron and Pip suspects Orlick, the surly journeyman who works at the forge. Biddy, a local girl, comes to the forge as housekeeper and he confides his dreams to her. These appear to be coming true when a London lawyer called Jaggers visits the forge and tells him that he has a mysterious benefactor and has 'great expectations' (Chapter 18, p. 138). He is to become a gentleman. Pip believes his patron is Miss Havisham, and already feels superior to his old friends at the forge as he sets off for London.

Pip arrives in Little Britain, near Newgate, where Jaggers has his office. It is dirty and sordid, but it is clear that Jaggers is a very effective criminal lawyer. Pip makes friends with Jaggers' clerk Wemmick and Herbert Pocket, a relation of Miss Havisham's. Pip learns to be a gentleman, and is uncomfortable when simple Joe comes to see him. Pip visits Satis House and later accompanies Estella

> **CONTEXT**
>
> This gloomy, menacing opening scene is based on the Kent marshes of Dickens' own early childhood, spent in Chatham and Rochester. The churchyard at Cooling near the Medway estuary is a likely source for the 'five little stone lozenges' (p. 3) that mark the graves of Pip's siblings. The last gibbeting took place in 1832.

CHECK THE FILM

David Lean's 1946 film has a memorable sequence of the early marsh scenes that captures the mood of the original text very well.

in London, but he only returns to the forge for his sister's funeral. He believes he is destined for Estella, but his relationship with her brings him no happiness. On his twenty-first birthday, Pip gets five hundred pounds and uses some of the money secretly to buy Herbert a partnership in a shipping firm. He becomes increasingly jealous of Estella's flirtation with a boorish gentleman called Drummle and witnesses a quarrel between her and Miss Havisham, who is dismayed at her lack of feeling. One stormy night a rough man visits Pip unannounced. It is Abel Magwitch, the convict that Pip helped on the marshes long ago. He was transported to Australia where he has made money sheep-farming. He has never forgotten Pip's action and he is responsible for Pip's 'great expectations'.

Pip is dismayed that all his fine dreams are based on the labour of a criminal and he feels unable to profit by it. He goes to Satis House to learn that Estella is to be married to Drummle. Magwitch is now in danger. The fellow convict he fought on the marsh, Compeyson, is in London. He and Magwitch are sworn enemies and it was Compeyson who tricked and deserted Miss Havisham. As Pip prepares with Herbert for Magwitch's escape, Miss Havisham invites him once more to Satis House. She asks forgiveness and agrees to help Herbert with a gift of money. As he leaves, her clothes catch fire. Although Pip attempts to save her, she is badly burnt and dies soon after. Orlick, who now works for Compeyson, nearly murders Pip but he is rescued in time to help Magwitch escape abroad. They try to board a steamer but are foiled by the police helped by Compeyson. In the ensuing struggle, Compeyson drowns and Magwitch is badly hurt. Pip has discovered that Estella is Magwitch's daughter. As Magwitch dies in prison, Pip tells him that she is alive and he loves her. Pip falls ill and Joe comes to London to nurse him. Pip can now see that Joe is 'a Christian gentle man' (Chapter 57, p. 463).

Pip returns to the forge intending to propose to Biddy but she has married Joe. Pip joins Herbert in his business abroad and prospers. After eleven years, he returns home and visits the ruins of Satis House for the last time. By chance he meets Estella there, now a widow and softened by her harsh marriage. Pip can see no shadow of another parting from her.

VOLUME I

CHAPTER 1

- Pip is surprised by an escaped convict in the village graveyard.

GLOSSARY

vittles 'victuals', meaning food

battery disused gun emplacement

gibbet public gallows where criminals were hanged on display

The novel begins by Philip Pirrip, the retrospective first person narrator, telling the reader how he came to call himself Pip. He then recounts his first memorable experience in the bleak marsh landscape of his childhood. Weeping among the graves of his parents and brothers, he is seized by a threatening man with a leg-iron. Discovering he lives with the local blacksmith, the man demands that Pip bring him food and a file, or his even more terrifying companion will seek Pip out and eat his heart and liver.

COMMENTARY

The opening chapter plunges the reader straight into a crisis of identity as Pip seeks to find out who he is and his place in an extremely inhospitable world. Pip's comic misreading of his parents' tombstone introduces the reader to some important themes in the novel: namely the idea of self-authorship and the making of an identity, the search for lost parentage and the misunderstanding of evidence generally. This windswept desolate place of mud, mist and water is like the world before creation when God divided the water from the dry land (see the opening chapter of Genesis in the Bible). In his search for his origins, Pip seems to have created 'a second father' (see Chapter 39, p. 320) in the convict who leaps up from among the graves, turns him upside down **metaphorically** as well as literally, and places him on his parents' tombstone. Throughout the novel, Pip will be haunted by his memory of this desolate place with its mist and cold winds, and return to it both physically and in his guilty thoughts. By blending a child's view of things with the more detached attitude of an adult narrator, Dickens creates a world of violence and humour which is very entertaining. This is important as in a serial the reader must be immediately engaged and encouraged to read on.

CHAPTER 2

- We learn about the stormy domestic life of the Gargery household.
- Pip steals some food and a file.

Pip returns home and is punished for being out late by his angry sister, 'Mrs Joe', who is a domestic tyrant. She intimidates both Pip and Joe, her kind but ineffectual husband who is the local village blacksmith. They are both forced to drink disgusting tar-water for 'bolting' (p. 12) their food. It's Christmas Eve and a warning gun tells them that a convict has escaped from the Hulks. Pip spends a bad night dreaming of the past day's extraordinary events. He gets up early and steals brandy and a pie from the pantry, and a file from the forge.

COMMENTARY

Humour and violence are combined in the black comedy of 'tickler' (p. 8), 'bringing-up by hand' (p. 7), the consequence of Pip hiding bread down his trouser-leg and the manner in which Mrs Joe attends to the needs of her family. Pip's home life seems little better than his experience in the churchyard. 'Bringing up by hand' is a repeated **motif** in the early chapters. It means bottle-fed rather than weaned from the breast but it is also a comic **pun**: Pip has been brought up by his sister's liberal use of 'tickler' rather than by any warmth and affection on her part. It is significant that we are not given any Christian name that would give her personality some human intimacy. The grotesque ideas of hunger, food and cannibalism and the 'young man' having Pip's 'heart and liver out' (Chapter 1, p. 5) are given a more comic treatment here with Mrs Joe's aggressive catering arrangements and the administration of the tar-water.

CHAPTER 3

- Pip feeds the convict and tells him of the other man.

Crossing the misty marshes, Pip surprises another man dressed like the first. Assuming this is the terrible young man he has been threatened with, he runs away. He finds his own cold and hungry convict who eats the food with animal desperation. Pip leaves him angrily filing off his fetter and vowing to hunt down the other man.

COMMENTARY

Again we have an adult reconstruction of a child's experience centred in a child's innocent world. Pip's guilty fears, his concern for the convict and the convict's own self-pity and anger are all well conveyed in this manner. By comparing the click in the convict's throat to the internal workings of a clock, Dickens is using an apt **simile** that allows us to understand the full complexity of the convict's emotions, which are accurately recorded by Pip as an observant child but could not be fully understood by him at that time. Pip's natural kindness for the cold, starving outcast is the beginning of a bond that will shape the plot. He provides the file that frees the convict but this act will also bind Pip to him irrevocably.

CHAPTER 4

- Christmas dinner at the forge is described.

Joe and Pip are made to go to church uncomfortably dressed in their best clothes while Mrs Joe prepares a splendid Christmas dinner. Mr and Mrs Hubble, Wopsle and Joe's uncle Pumblechook are the invited guests. Pip is made to feel guilty and unhappy by the assembled company and compared to a pig. He is in continual suspense that his theft will be discovered. Events move towards a climax when Pumblechook drinks from the brandy bottle which Pip has inadvertently diluted with tar-water and Mrs Joe goes to get the missing pork-pie. Pip panics and makes a run for the door only to find himself confronted by a soldier holding out some handcuffs.

COMMENTARY

This is a horrible **parody** of normal Christmas festivities where everyone but Joe is unkind to Pip, who is abused and made to eat the worst food. We are introduced to some new comic characters.

GLOSSARY

monumental Crusaders effigies of knights on tombs with their legs crossed were thought to have gone to the crusades

penitentials clothes worn to show sorrow for sin

Accoucheur male midwife

thrown open the church is not open to Wopsle as a career because he is from the lower classes

Medium someone capable of moving objects through the power of unseen spiritual forces

Pumblechook's punishment by drinking tar-water is a good example of poetic justice. Although Mrs Joe fawns on him, he is a glutton and a bully so it is entirely appropriate that he should drink her dreadful medicine. The fact that it is Pip, his victim, who is responsible, adds still more to our comic pleasure. This theme of punishment and retribution is given darker expression by the sudden arrival of the soldiers bearing a pair of handcuffs. The chapter ends with the surprise and suspense that is important for a successful serial.

GLOSSARY

Hob and nob a convivial toast

sluice-gate device to control the flow of water and drain the marshes

CHAPTER 5

- The soldiers hunt for and recapture the convicts.

Pumblechook liberally entertains the soldiers with the wine given to Mrs Joe for Christmas while Joe mends the handcuffs. Christmas at the forge has suddenly become quite jovial at the expense of the fugitives on the cold marshes. Along with Wopsle, Joe takes Pip with the soldiers in the search for the escaped convicts. They are discovered fighting in a ditch. Pip's convict has stopped the other from getting away. Pip tries to reassure him that he is not responsible for his recapture. Responding to his beseeching look, Pip's convict confesses to the thefts from the forge before being returned to the Hulks and so saves Pip from punishment.

COMMENTARY

CONTEXT

'In the name of the king' (p. 30) refers to George III: the novel is set in pre-Victorian times.

Joe's Christian forgiveness of a 'poor miserable fellow-creatur' (p. 40) contrasts with the pleasure others get from the hunting down and recapture of the convicts. By calling the Hulk a 'wicked Noah's ark' (p. 40) the narrator uses a suggestive **metaphor** that links up with the primeval description of the marshes in the opening chapter. Noah's ark saved the animals from the flood for the future. This ship locks away its inmates from the world. Noah's animals went in 'two by two' in mutual accord; these convicts are treated like animals but they clearly hate each other. So a religious, biblical reference is qualified by a more modern sense of nature as cruel, and of men struggling against each other for survival and no better than beasts. We note that Pip's convict makes much of calling the other a 'gentleman' which seems odd in this context.

CHAPTER 6

- The hunting party returns home.
- Pip's confused conscience is described.

Pip feels no remorse for stealing from his sister but he does feel he should confess to Joe. He decides against it for fear of losing his only friend. There is a comic argument between Wopsle and Pumblechook as to how the convict broke in.

COMMENTARY

Pip's decision to keep a guilty secret marks the beginning of his loss of innocence and eventual separation from Joe. The substance of the novel we have just begun is going to be Pip's confession and only in Chapter 57 (see pp. 468–9) will the issue of Pip's moral cowardice over the theft for the convict be finally addressed. This will form part of the complex **closure** of the fiction.

CHAPTER 7

- Education and literacy are discussed.
- Pip and Joe converse round the fire.
- The return of Mrs Joe and Pumblechook from market-day.
- We learn of Miss Havisham's strange request.

A year after the convict's escape and recapture, Pip describes his education in the useless school kept by Wopsle's great-aunt while he waits to be apprenticed to Joe. He writes a comically inept letter to Joe and concludes from the response that Joe cannot read or write.

Mark Antony's oration from Shakespeare's *Julius Caesar*

Collins William Collins (1721–59), English poet

purple leptic Joe's attempt at 'apoplectic'

back-falls a wrestling term

Mooncalfs idiots

CONTEXT

Wopsle's great aunt runs a Dame School. These provided the only education open to poor children in most parts of the country before state provision and were generally very inadequate.

Joe tells Pip about his own childhood and the reasons why he endures his wife's domineering ways without complaint. Mrs Joe returns from town with Pumblechook in great excitement. Miss Havisham, a rich, eccentric, local recluse has expressed a wish for a boy to go and play in her house. Pip is scrubbed and dressed in his best clothes before being sent off with Pumblechook.

COMMENTARY

This is a chapter full of sentiment and comedy. The education theme is important to the novel as a whole. It was introduced in the first chapter with Pip attempting to decipher the family tombstones and is developed here. Pip begins to discover his inherently superior intelligence to Joe's: this is revealed in the narrator's tone of superiority when describing Joe's literary efforts, his awkward speech habits and his comically confused vocabulary, but this chapter also demonstrates Joe's innate moral sensitivity and goodness. Joe's description of his childhood compares with Pip's now, and the focus on reading and writing shows literacy and education as the means by which individuals develop their social identity and are able to rise in the world. The return of Mrs Joe and Pumblechook introduces a fresh development in the plot and the theme of 'expectations'.

CHAPTER 8

GLOSSARY

beggar my neighbour a card game for two where the winner takes all

- Pip goes on his first visit to Satis House.

Pip has breakfast with Pumblechook who bullies him with tasks of mental arithmetic before taking him to see Miss Havisham. A young girl called Estella lets him at in the gate, leaving the indignant Pumblechook outside. Satis House is a grand, crumbling mansion with a neglected garden and a disused brewery in the grounds. Miss Havisham is old but she sits in the decayed remnants of a wedding dress in a candlelit dressing-room where all the clocks have stopped at twenty to nine. Everything around her suggests that, amid the preparations for her wedding, time has suddenly stopped for Miss

Havisham too. She says that her heart is broken. Pip plays cards with Estella who is unkind to him, mocking his speech, coarse hands and thick boots. Miss Havisham takes a pride in Estella's beauty and cruelty. Left to eat a meal alone, Pip weeps; as he wanders round the disused brewery he imagines he sees Miss Havisham hanging from a beam. Eventually Estella lets him go, enjoying his pain and humiliation.

CONTEXT

The local town is based on Dickens' childhood memories of Rochester, and Satis House on Gad's Hill, a house he admired as a child and bought in 1856.

COMMENTARY

Pip's ordeals continue but this time in a world of upper-class decay. He feels Estella's taunts keenly, for his sister's rough treatment has left him very sensitive. Although the dark and gloomy Satis House seems far removed from the squalor of the Hulks and the bleakness of the marshes, there are significant links with the opening chapters. A cold wind blows here too. Estella gives Pip a meal, but in a very different spirit from that in which he fed the convict in Chapter 3 (see also the meals described in Chapters 2, 4, 22, 26 and 40).

Pip is introduced to the world of class distinction by Estella's taunts about his hands and speech. The name 'Estella' suggests 'star-like' and from the beginning she is depicted as being cold, distant and unobtainable. There is obvious **symbolism** in the way she carries a lighted candle about the gloomy house like 'a star' (p. 59) and moves around the brewery's disused galleries 'as if she were going out into the sky' (p. 64). The card game is also **symbolically** named, for much of the novel describes a ruthless world of selfish acquisition and 'beggaring one's neighbours' (see Wemmick in London later on the need for 'portable property', p. 409). So, too, is the name of the house: 'Satis' means 'enough'; as Pip remarks, this is a curious name for a house. Estella's explanation is that anyone lucky enough to own the house could want nothing else: 'They must have been easily satisfied in those days' (p. 56). This notion of the emptiness of possessions, which is to be such an important theme in the novel, is also underlined by the meaning concealed in Miss Havisham's name. This also 'means more than it says' (p. 56) for 'Havisham' suggests 'have a sham'. The vision of Miss Havisham hanging from a beam echoes the images of the gibbet and hanging pirate in Chapter 1 and associates her with death and self-destruction. The bleak, elemental landscape of the marshes and the splendid decline of Satis House both share imagery of **gothic** terror and intimidation. Like the interior of the house, the overgrown garden and the disused brewery are suggestive of Miss Havisham's own decayed and barren, misused body.

CHAPTER 9

- Pip tells an elaborate lie.
- Pip first becomes dissatisfied with his origins.

On his return home, Pip is bullied into an account of his day at Satis House. Instead of telling the truth, he invents an improbable story involving a black velvet coach, games with flags and swords, food from golden plates and four huge dogs eating veal cutlets from a silver basket. Rather than admit his ignorance, Pumblechook goes along with the story. Later Pip admits his lie to a shocked Joe who says he will never improve himself by lying. Pip goes to bed thinking how common Estella would think his life at the forge.

COMMENTARY

That Pip's invention could be believed by the credulous adults at the forge shows the gulf between the lives of the rich and the poor at this time. But this episode also draws our attention to the relative claims of truth and fiction. Pip's story is a lie yet tells a kind of truth. It is no stranger than the reality of Satis House; it is truthful to the mood of the experience and some events, like Pip's humiliating meal, are recounted in a disguised form. It may be that Pip introduces the dogs into his story because he has been treated 'as if I were a dog in disgrace' (p. 62). Already he is using his imagination to create consoling dreams and Joe gives a warning of the dangers of doing this. The chapter ends with the **imagery** of chains with its suggestion of bondage (see Chapter 13 for a development of this idea).

CHAPTER 10

- Pip seeks to improve his education.
- There is a mysterious stranger at the Three Jolly Bargemen with a file and two 'sweltering' pound notes.

Pip seeks help from Biddy, another young orphan like himself who works at Wopsle's great-aunt's school. Returning from another unsatisfactory evening there, Pip calls for Joe at the village inn, to find him and Wopsle talking to a stranger who shows a particular interest in Pip's identity. In a manner concealed to all but Pip, the stranger stirs his drink with what Pip recognises as Joe's stolen file. He gives Pip two well-used pound notes disguised as wrapping-paper round a shilling and departs before they can be returned.

COMMENTARY

This is the first of several occasions when the criminal world of Pip's convict re-emerges to remind him of the past and disconcert him (see Chapters 20, 28 and 32). The money is a clue as to the source of Pip's later 'expectations', and in Chapter 39 Pip attempts to return to Magwitch two 'clean and new' pound notes (p. 318).

GLOSSARY

nevvy nephew

Blue Blazes an oath

having professional occasion Wopsle is showing off his knowledge as a church clerk

Richard the Third play by Shakespeare

sweltering soiled and much used

CHAPTER 11

- Pip goes on a second visit to Satis House.
- Pip meets the Pocket relations and has a fight with a pale young gentleman.

It is Miss Havisham's birthday and her greedy relations have gathered to pay their respects. They mention another, Matthew Pocket, who refuses to come. Pip also meets a forbidding man on the stairs. He is shown into a dark, disused dining room with closed-up windows. On the long table there is a mouldy wedding cake full of spiders and beetles. Miss Havisham says that she will lie

GLOSSARY

deep trimmings mourning garments

sal volatile smelling salts to revive the fainting

staylace binding for a corset

giant a reference to Cronos in Greek mythology who ate his own children

CHECK THE NET
For more on the matter of women's property and Miss Havisham's particular situation at this time see:
http://www.umd. umich.edu/casl/ hum/eng/classes/ 434/geweb/

there when she is dead, her relations around her, and the curse will be complete. We learn that she was to be married on this day, many years ago. Later Pip wanders in the derelict garden and meets a young boy who challenges him to a fight. He is comically inept and Pip easily beats him, much to Estella's satisfaction. She kisses him in a patronising manner but Pip feels sorry for the young gentleman, who was brave and took his beating in good part.

COMMENTARY

The gloomy unchanging rituals of Satis House are explored further. Everything around Miss Havisham is condemned, like her body, to sterility, disuse and decay and the distorted growth in the garden (pp. 80, 90) picks up on the **imagery** of imprisoned bulbs in Pumblechook's shop (Chapter 8, p. 53) and Wemmick's greenhouse 'plants' in chapter 32. The shocking notion of Miss Havisham lying dead on the great dining table, for her relatives to feast on, continues the notion of cannibalism that we have encountered in the opening chapters. Miss Havisham's contempt for her relatives prepares us for her use of Pip to torment them later (Chapter 19). The great decaying bride-cake is a powerful **symbol** of her morbid and poisoned mind, and Estella's pleasure at the fight anticipates Mrs Joe's much more violent hysteria when Joe and Orlick do battle in Chapter 15.

GLOSSARY
Old Clem St Clement was the protector of blacksmiths
indentures legal documents binding an apprentice

CHAPTER 12

- Pip pays more visits to Satis House.
- There are debates on Pip's future at the forge.
- Miss Havisham asks to see Joe about Pip's apprenticeship and Mrs Joe goes on the rampage.

Pip is guilty about the fight but the visits to Satis House are unaffected and continue on a frequent and regular basis. He pushes Miss Havisham around in a wheelchair for hours, often singing 'Old Clem', a blacksmith's work-song. Mrs Joe and Pumblechook delight in speculations concerning Pip's possible reward. Pip now confides in Biddy rather than Joe who is unenthusiastic about him leaving the forge. Miss Havisham notices that Pip is growing up and asks to see Joe with his indentures, much to Mrs Joe's annoyance and pique.

COMMENTARY

This is a transition chapter covering the best part of a year and describes Pip's new routine at Satis House. Pip's confession of excessive guilt over the fight with 'the pale young gentleman' (p. 90) and the bleakly comic description of his continuing persecution by his sister and Pumblechook achieve their effect through the sophisticated language of the older narrator looking back. The shame over his colourful lie (Chapter 9) increases his alienation from Joe and there is a retrospective sadness over Biddy's affection towards him at this time and his own lack of perception concerning his feelings. Signs of Pip's insidious corruption and class discontent become evident, both at the forge where Mrs Joe and Pumblechook have 'great expectations' for him and seek to overrule Joe's wish that he follow the traditional blacksmith's craft, and in the artificial candlelight of Satis House where Pip's thoughts are confused by Estella's capricious, unpredictable moods.

 CHECK THE NET

There is some discussion of blacksmiths and the significance of this work in the novel at **http://www.umd. umich.edu/casl/ hum/eng/classes/ 434/geweb/** under 'Work and Social Class'.

CHAPTER 13

- We witness a comic interview between Miss Havisham and Joe.
- Joe receives twenty-five guineas for Pip's apprenticeship which mollifies Mrs Joe considerably.
- There are general celebrations which Pip does not share.

Joe visits Mrs Havisham uncomfortably dressed in his Sunday clothes. Pip is very embarrassed at his appearance and clumsy manners at Satis House. Joe insists on conducting his interview through Pip without addressing Miss Havisham directly and gets very muddled in his speech. Miss Havisham can see he is a decent man, however, and gives Pip a premium, dismissing him and telling Joe to expect no more. Joe shows unexpected diplomatic tact in handing over the money to Mrs Joe to soothe her hurt pride. Pip is taken to the Town Hall to sign his indentures. His mood is gloomy while his sister and her friends celebrate at the Blue Boar.

GLOSSARY

Great Seal of England it was kept in a big straw bag

premium initial fee that a new apprentice paid to his master

Rantipole madman

bound legal term for 'becoming an apprentice'

fired a rick burned a haystack

hardbake toffee

The Commercials commercial travellers

O Lady Fair a popular song

COMMENTARY

Whenever Joe speaks there is always a contrast between his clumsy, often comical, expressions and the gentle, decent, even wise, content of his speech (see his interview with Pip in London, Chapter 27, his advice to Pip, Chapter 15, or the earlier discussion of his family life, Chapter 7). Compare this interview with that with Jaggers in Chapter 18. Although very different in tone, both show Joe's indifference to money and his natural unselfishness. However, he does lie to Mrs Joe about Miss Havisham's money, something he has warned Pip not to do (Chapter 9) and so draws attention to the complex relationship between truth and fiction. Note the guilty, criminal feelings that still cling to Pip. There is much made of the notion of his being 'bound' that links Pip to his convict associations as well as his reluctance to become a blacksmith.

CHAPTER 14

- Pip is unhappy in his apprenticeship: 'restlessly aspiring discontented me' (p. 108).

After his experience of Satis House, Pip is ashamed of the forge. He cannot put Estella from his mind and thinks how she would despise his life of honest toil.

COMMENTARY

This is a retrospective chapter as the narrator looks back at his newly acquired class consciousness.

CHAPTER 15

- Pip continues to try and educate himself.
- Orlick has a fight with Joe.
- Pip visits Satis House and Mrs Joe is violently attacked.

Pip has now outgrown the village school and his attempts to teach Joe end in failure. Joe advises against another visit to Satis House but Pip is determined. Joe's journeyman, surly Dolge Orlick, demands a half-holiday, too, and when Mrs Joe interferes a violent fight ensues. Joe wins easily but Mrs Joe has hysterics and has to be carried up to bed. Pip arrives at Satis House to find Estella has gone away to become a lady. Miss Havisham seems gratified by his disappointment. He agrees to visit her every year on his birthday. Meeting Wopsle in town, he stays on to hear him act the story of George Barnwell in Pumblechook's parlour. Barnwell was an apprentice, like Pip, who went bad and murdered his uncle. Pip is made to feel very guilty by Pumblechook who tells him to 'take warning' (p. 117). Returning to the village with Wopsle, he comes across Orlick on the road and hears the guns signalling the escape of a convict. At the forge, Mrs Joe is found crippled by a mighty blow to the head.

> **CONTEXT**
>
> George Barnwell (p.117) was a popular play by George Lillo (1693–1739) about an apprentice who commits murder and is hanged. Sarah Millwood was Barnwell's lover and accomplice.

COMMENTARY

The fight is comically alarming, not for itself but the effect it has on Mrs Joe. This suggests strong repression, maybe of a sexual nature, which the violence between the men releases in her. As a Victorian writer, Dickens would be unwilling to reveal the matter openly. Our attention is drawn to the parallel between this fight and the one between Pip and the other young boy which gratified Estella so much.

Joe is right that Miss Havisham suspects Pip 'wanted something' (p. 110) and her warning that 'you'll get nothing' (p. 116) is one that he should heed. By agreeing to visit Miss Havisham on a regular annual basis, Pip's relationship has now become similar to that of the Pocket relations. Wopsle's performance is the first of several that Pip is audience to (see his Hamlet, Chapter 31, and pantomime character, Chapter 47). Once again Pip is made to feel guilty and potentially criminal in nature and this is emphasised by the firing of the guns on the marshes that recall memories of the opening chapters. The effect is to make the revelation of Mrs Joe's injury both shocking and curiously inevitable: a dramatic conclusion to this weekly part.

CHAPTER 16

- The leg-iron and the events leading up to the attack on Mrs Joe are described.
- Mrs Joe has a strange desire to see Orlick.

Pip feels that he is somehow responsible for what has happened. This is reinforced by the discovery of the weapon her assailant used. It is an old leg-iron and he is convinced that it is the one from his convict but still feels unable to tell Joe the whole story. Pip suspects Orlick or the stranger with the file (Chapter 10). Detectives come from London but fail to solve the case. Mrs Joe is now brain damaged and unable to communicate easily. However, she makes signs that she wants to see Orlick. Pip hopes that she will denounce him but, instead, she is pleased to see him. Biddy now takes her place in the household.

CONTEXT
Bow Street men (p. 112) were an early detective force. The Bow Street Runners were disbanded in 1829.

COMMENTARY

We have a fresh mystery and several possible solutions. The leg-iron does seem to make Pip guilty by association. It carries the taint of criminality and, because of his old secret, it implicates him. He has unknowingly provided the weapon and must harbour resentment against his sister. Mrs Joe is now a spent force and with Biddy in charge, the forge will become a gentler, more secure place. Pip will have less excuse to leave. Mrs Joe's placatory behaviour to Orlick has no obvious explanation but remains a haunting enigma. It suggests some kind of masochistic dependency on Mrs Joe's part and her attraction to violence. Her sign of the hammer on the slate recalls the comedy of Pip's letter to Joe in Chapter 7 but the mood is now much darker.

CHAPTER 17

- Life at the forge continues.
- Pip tells Biddy of his ambitions and love for Estella.
- Orlick also shows an interest in Biddy.

Pip continues in his apprenticeship and his short annual visits to see Miss Havisham. He admires Biddy but is unable to shake off his obsession with Estella. On a Sunday afternoon walk on the marshes he tells Biddy that he wants to be a gentleman and why. Biddy gives him sensible advice. She tells him that Estella is not worthy of his love and he should not live his life to please her. He wishes that he could love Biddy but she says he never will. Returning, they meet Orlick who starts to follow them. Biddy tells Pip that Orlick likes her, much to Pip's indignation and annoyance. He still hopes that somehow Miss Havisham will make his fortune.

COMMENTARY

Pip's dialogue with Biddy is full of subtle implication and some **irony**. We are led to believe that Pip likes Biddy more than he cares to admit to himself and that she, in a much less confused way, is fond of him. She mocks his presumption that she would marry him and shows remarkable forbearance at his insensitive treatment of her. He is full of self-pity; she genuinely pities him. She is much more realistic and self-controlled in her emotions than he is and can see his faults. We are not given access to Biddy's thoughts and feelings; we can only infer them from Pip's insensitive point of view but her whole attitude and behaviour towards him is a pointed contrast to Estella's. The manner in which Estella is associated with the landscape shows that, for Pip, she is an ideal image and vague aspiration rather than a real person. Pip's anger at Orlick indicates his own rather confused feelings towards Biddy.

CHECK THE BOOK

Julian Moynahan's article, 'The Hero's Guilt: The Case of Great Expectations', most conveniently to be found in Norman Page (ed.) *Charles Dickens: Hard Times, Great Expectations and Our Mutual Friend: A Casebook* (1979), has a fascinating discussion on the leg-iron as a symbol of Pip's sense of guilt and culpability. Moynahan also suggests that Orlick is a character who seems to act out Pip's suppressed feelings of revenge for his sister and his feelings towards Biddy.

well and truly try the oath made by a jury

Brag is a good dog, but Holdfast is better silence is better than speech

ekervally Joe's attempt at 'equally'

CHAPTER 18

- Jaggers upstages Wopsle at the Three Jolly Bargemen.
- Jaggers interviews Pip and Joe at the forge.
- We learn of mixed emotions of all at the forge at the news of Pip's expectations.

It is now the fourth year of Pip's apprenticeship. One Saturday night a stranger enters the Three Jolly Bargemen. Wopsle is reading from the local newspaper and giving one of his performances as the coroner in a murder case. The company have been convinced that the accused is guilty but the man suggests otherwise. He is Jaggers, a London lawyer with a bullying manner, and he makes Wopsle look foolish. Pip recognises him as the man on the stairs he once met at Satis House (Chapter 11). Later he asks Joe if he is willing to release Pip from his indentures because he has a secret benefactor and 'great expectations' (p. 138). He must always bear the name of Pip and must not enquire after the identity of his patron until that person chooses to reveal it. He must go to London and learn to be a gentleman. Matthew Pocket is to be his tutor. Pip is given money for new clothes and other expenses and is to go to London in a week's time. Joe refuses compensation for the loss of his apprentice and, upset by his manner, threatens to fight Jaggers so he leaves without further delay. Both Joe and Biddy seem sad and Pip cannot understand why he does not feel more elated at his good fortune.

COMMENTARY

Of course, Pip assumes that the source of his good fortune is Miss Havisham. He has seen Jaggers at Satis House and heard mention of Matthew Pocket there (Chapter 11). However, the reader may be less inclined to forget Miss Havisham's calculating, spiteful ways, despite this strong circumstantial evidence. Jaggers has also demonstrated the danger of making easy assumptions earlier at The Three Jolly Bargemen. The contrast and conflict between Joe and Jaggers is significant. Jaggers' verbal bullying and legal caution are forced on the defensive by Joe's inarticulate rage. When Jaggers talks of being 'paid for his services' (p. 139) we recognise a new kind of relationship and different sort of 'guardian' to Joe whose ties to Pip transcend money (see also Pip and Joe receiving Pip's premium by Miss Havisham in Chapter 13). The narrator's talk of 'dear good faithful tender Joe' (p. 141) touching his arm long ago draws our attention to the retrospective nature of the narrative which is written by an older, wiser Pip looking back sadly over his early life. The end of the chapter shows him already condescending to his family but feeling lonely.

CHAPTER 19

- Pip feels a patronising superiority towards the forge and the village.
- Pip is rebuked by Biddy and measured for a new suit.
- The transformation in attitude that money can achieve is explored.
- Pip has dinner with Pumblechook, and says farewell to Miss Havisham.
- Pip finally departs on the London coach.

Pip has a last walk on the marshes and tries to dismiss all memories of the convict. He suggests to Biddy that Joe might now be better educated for a higher station in life but she says that he is a proud man, secure in his position and quite content where he is. Pip says that she is envious and she says he is unjust. Trabb, the local tailor, receives Pip very deferentially although his boy is less impressed. Pumblechook assumes that Miss Havisham is the source of Pip's prospects and claims some of the responsibility for his good fortune. He feeds and flatters Pip excessively, suggesting he might put money in the business. Miss Havisham uses Pip's visit to torment Sarah Pocket. Pip's departure is constrained. He departs alone for fear of being seen with Joe in his new clothes and later regrets it.

COMMENTARY

The dignified and caring attitude of Biddy and Joe is contrasted with the self-seeking selfishness of those who wish to use or flatter

GLOSSARY

The rich man and the Kingdom of Heaven 'It is easier for a camel to go through the eye of a needle, than for a rich man to enter into the kingdom of God.' (Matthew, 19:24)

oncommon plump suddenly

Mother Hubbard's dog in the nursery rhyme, Mother Hubbard goes to many shops to buy clothes and accessories for her dog

flip a hot alcoholic drink

an old shoe symbol of good luck

CONTEXT

By the time that Dickens wrote *Great Expectations*, train travel had superseded the stagecoach, thus dating Pip's journey to the earlier part of the nineteenth century.

Pip for their own ends. Notice that Pumblechook's servile '*May* I? *May* I?' (p. 143) and his behaviour to Pip over their meal together are in marked contrast to his earlier behaviour at the Christmas dinner in Chapter 4. Pip's snobbishness is partly his own weakness but it is encouraged by the attitude of others. Pip is not blind to Miss Havisham's cruelty to Sarah Pocket but sees her now as a 'fairy godmother' (p. 157) rather than 'the Witch of the place' (p. 85). The **motif** of the finger post is suggestive of the Dick Whittington fairy tale; Pip's story could be viewed as an ironic commentary on and reversal of this traditional story of 'rags to riches'. It points back to the village, the marsh and the forge, not forward to London.

VOLUME II

CHAPTER 20

- We hear of Pip's first experiences of London.
- Pip visits Jaggers' chambers in 'Little Britain', Newgate and Smithfield.

On his arrival, Pip is shown into Jaggers' gloomy office near the law courts where the death masks of two hanged criminals gaze down on him from the wall. Taking a walk, he finds the meat-market of Smithfield disgusting and Newgate Prison sordid. The trials are on and he is given a guided tour of the prison yard where criminals are punished and hanged. Everywhere he sees evidence of Jaggers' power as a criminal lawyer. Jaggers finally arrives, bullies potential clients and dismisses a comically unreliable witness. He gives Pip money and instructions to stay with young Herbert Pocket at Barnard's Inn for the weekend before going on to his father's house.

COMMENTARY

Significantly, Pip's first experiences of his 'great expectations' are associated with crime, butchery and punishment. The scene at Smithfield 'all asmear with filth and fat' (p. 165) recalls

---

GLOSSARY

Little Britain a street near St Paul's and the Law Courts

minister of justice Pip refers, with irony, to the gatekeeper of Newgate Prison

Cag-Maggerth 'cag-mag' means rotten meat, so all lawyers save Jaggers are no good

Cock Robin a nursery rhyme

Barnard's Inn one of the old Inns of Court, no longer used

Outrunning the constable spending too much

Pumblechook's dire predictions for Pip's fate at the hands of Dunstable the butcher if he had been born 'a four-footed Squeaker' (p. 27) in Chapter 4. It is clear that Jaggers is a lawyer without scruples or feeling. The death masks are a kind of **motif** that reappears whenever Pip enters Jaggers' office. Also the gallows in Newgate Yard link up with the gibbet on the marshes and Pip's vision of a hanging Miss Havisham in the brewery at Satis House (see Chapter 8).

> **CONTEXT**
>
> The last public hanging in Newgate was in 1868. The invitation to see four prisoners 'killed in a row' (p. 166) is not an exaggeration. To execute four to six prisoners at any one time was quite usual.

CHAPTER 21

- Pip goes with Wemmick to Barnard's Inn, a very dismal place.
- Pip discovers Herbert Pocket to be the 'pale young gentleman' (p. 90) he beat long ago.

Pip notices that Jaggers' clerk, Wemmick, has a very wooden appearance and a straight mouth that gives him the appearance of smiling when he is not. He also wears much mourning jewellery and is surprised when, on parting, Pip offers to shake hands with him. Barnard's Inn has fallen into decay and seems very like a graveyard. Pip narrowly avoids injury from a decrepit, falling window and discovers that Herbert is the young boy he fought at Satis House.

COMMENTARY

As in the graveyard scene that opens the book, Pip misinterprets information in a London new to him; he thinks that Barnard's Inn is a grand hotel and is quickly disillusioned. Through Wemmick's cautious formality, Pip learns that London manners are different from the country. The **motif** of hand shaking recalls Pumblechook's '*May* I? *May* I?' (Chapter 19, p. 143) and the comic accident with the falling window is yet another variant on the theme of crime and punishment. The miserable, rotten state of Barnard's Inn is reminiscent of Satis House, a link with the past that is reinforced by the reappearance of Herbert (see Chapter 11).

CHAPTER 22

GLOSSARY

a Tarter a fierce person

a crack thing a good profession

'Change The Royal Exchange, centre for marine insurance in London

- Pip has his first lesson on becoming a gentleman.
- Herbert tells the story of Miss Havisham's early life.
- Herbert takes Pip to his family home at Hammersmith.

Pip's first assessments of Herbert are favourable. Although he is poor and is indecisive about his future prospects, he is cheerful and has the unmistakable air of a gentleman. He decides to call Pip 'Handel' and, tactfully, begins to improve his table manners over dinner. His family is related to Miss Havisham and he tells how, long ago, when she was a young, rich heiress, she was jilted on her wedding day by a heartless suitor who, with the help of her half-brother, took much of her money. Her response was to lay waste the house, suspend time and live as a recluse. Only Matthew Pocket foresaw the danger and warned Miss Havisham. He was dismissed and has never visited the house since. Herbert knows nothing of Estella except that she has been brought up by Miss Havisham to take her revenge on the male sex. After the weekend, Herbert takes Pip to Matthew Pocket's house where he finds considerable domestic confusion.

COMMENTARY

This is an important chapter for the plot because Herbert, in the form of a flashback to events that took place well before Pip's story begins, gives the reader crucial information that Pip could not know. (See Chapters 42 and 50–1 for a similar use of this device where Magwitch and Jaggers fill in the details of events long ago.) As readers, we now have mysteries to unravel: what has happened to Miss Havisham's brother and lover? Who are Estella's parents? This chapter also develops an important theme in the novel. This is the significance of being a gentleman and what attributes a true gentleman should possess (see **Themes: Gentlemen and gentle men**). Pip is renamed and begins to learn to become a gentleman; although poor, Herbert, like his father, seems to be an instinctive gentleman, while Miss Havisham's suitor may have all the social graces and external appearance of one but is not a true gentleman.

CHECK THE BOOK

Robin Gilmour discusses this aspect of *Great Expectations* at some length in his book *The Idea of the Gentleman in the Victorian Novel* (1981).

The point is underlined by Mathew Pocket's reported opinion: 'no man who was not a true gentleman at heart, ever was, since the world began, a true gentleman in manner … no varnish can hide the grain in the wood' (p. 181). Herbert's tactful instruction on appropriate table manners continues to develop the thematic treatment of food and eating noted earlier (See Chapters 3, 4, 8, 19, 26, 27 and 40).

CHAPTER 23

- We learn of the domestic turmoil and disorder of the Pocket household.

We are introduced to Matthew Pocket, his wife and their large household. Matthew earns his living as a tutor and his domestic affairs are in a permanent state of crisis because of the incompetence of his wife. She feels that she has been denied her true social status and that family duties are beneath her. Accordingly the servants run everything with comically disastrous consequences. We meet Drummle and Startop, Pip's fellow lodgers.

COMMENTARY

This chapter is something of a comic interlude, although the Pocket household is another example of a dysfunctional family to compare with Mrs Joe's bringing up 'by hand' (p. 7) and Miss Havisham's perverse upbringing of Estella. Belinda Pocket's obsession with gentility is an absurd **caricature** of Pip's wish to become a gentleman. These scenes at the Pocket house, like those at the Dame School in Pip's childhood or those at Estella's residence at Richmond later, are not developed very much. This may be because of the constraints of weekly serialisation. Monthly parts would have allowed Dickens more space to elaborate these comic characters. Matthew Pocket's gesture of attempting to lift himself up by his hair, like his wife's constant dropping of her handkerchief, are the theatrical gestures by which we learn to identify them (see **Characterisation**).

 CHECK THE FILM

Note that David Lean's version, along with most others, tends to ignore these Hammersmith scenes. Does this mean they are less valuable for the reader of the text?

CHAPTER 24

- Pip's education proceeds.
- There are financial dealings with Jaggers and Wemmick on 'portable property'.

Pip decides to live with Herbert in London and requests money from Jaggers for furniture. He is unnerved by Jaggers' aggressive, interrogatory manner. Wemmick explains that this is part of his guardian's professional skill and shows Pip round the chambers and Jaggers at work in the court. Wemmick explains that his jewellery is 'portable property' (p. 201) given to him by condemned criminals, and invites Pip to visit his house in Walworth. He also says that when he dines with Jaggers, Pip will see 'a wild beast tamed' (p. 202).

COMMENTARY

Jaggers questions Pip in a style that is reminiscent of Pumplechook's arithmetical inquisition when Pip was a child (Chapter 8, p. 54). Wemmick's stress on the need to get hold of 'portable property' and his ghoulish method of obtaining it by exploiting condemned criminals are darkly comic but also reveal city life to be a constant struggle for survival. We remember Estella and Pip playing 'beggar my neighbour' in Chapter 8. Jaggers is a dedicated professional at all times but Wemmick shows a warmer side to his character towards the end of the chapter. His remarks on Jaggers' housekeeper hint of mysteries to come.

GLOSSARY

Britannia metal inferior metal made to look like silver

CHAPTER 25

- Pip's life at Hammersmith and London.
- The Pocket relations visit him.
- Pip goes to Wemmick's castle at Walworth.

Pip's companions Drummle and Startop are compared, greatly to Drummle's disadvantage. The other Pockets (see Chapter 11) fawn on Pip, assuming that his expectations come from Miss Havisham. Pip takes up Wemmick's invitation and discovers that he lives in a wooden cottage made to look like a miniature castle complete with flagstaff, drawbridge and small cannon. He is devoted to his aged father who is very deaf. Pip learns that Jaggers knows nothing of this and sees that Wemmick lives a double life.

COMMENTARY

Drummle's surly character and habit of creeping behind the others when they go rowing link him by association with Orlick despite his superior station in life. The Walworth episode is delightful comedy but also makes a serious point. Wemmick can only maintain his humanity by keeping his work and private life completely separated. His 'Walworth' personality is completely different from his 'Little Britain' one. This is **symbolised** by the increasing rigidity of his mouth as he returns with Pip to London. The firing of 'Stinger', although farcical, is also a reminder of the warning guns on the marshes long ago.

> **CONTEXT**
>
> At this time Walworth was a village outside London, just as Wemmick's domestic personality is separated from his working one.

CHAPTER 26

- Pip endures an uncomfortable evening with Jaggers.
- Jaggers displays his mysterious housekeeper and judgement on Drummle.

Pip, Startop and Drummle are invited to Jaggers' gloomy house in Soho where all hospitality is strictly controlled. Jaggers shows great pride in exhibiting the scarred wrist of his cowed housekeeper, Molly, and boasting of her strength. He admires Drummle as 'one of the true sort' (p. 217) and encourages his boorishness. The evening ends in bad temper and disorder.

> **CONTEXT**
>
> The 'Witches' cauldron' (p. 212) is a reference to Shakespeare's *Macbeth*. Lady Macbeth guiltily washes her hands like Jaggers in her sleep-walking scene.

COMMENTARY

This tense dinner party contrasts with Wemmick's warm sociability and good-natured banter with 'the Aged' (Chapter 25). It emphasises Jaggers' complete professional detachment. His final challenge to

Pip at the end of the chapter – 'You know what I am, don't you?' (p. 217) – is a challenge to the reader, too, for his character is a complete enigma. His pride in Molly is an unresolved mystery and his interest in Drummle suggests he sees a potential criminal in him. However, the compulsive washing which begins and ends the chapter also implies some strain and guilt in Jaggers' way of life.

CHAPTER 27

- Joe makes an unsuccessful visit to London.
- Pip receives news from home and an invitation to Satis House.

Pip receives a letter from Biddy announcing Joe's impending visit to London with disquiet. The meeting is very constrained because of Joe's social unease and Pip's snobbish anxiety. Pip learns that Wopsle has come to London to start a new career as an actor, and that Pumblechook is claiming to be Pip's intimate friend. He also discovers that Joe brings a message from Satis House; Estella has returned and wishes to see him. Joe leaves in awkward discomfiture but not before giving a dignified farewell. He will not come again but Pip is always welcome at the forge where Joe can be his true self.

COMMENTARY

This chapter maintains a skilful mix of humour and **pathos**. We can measure how far Pip has changed in his attitude to Joe. His servant, 'the avenging phantom' (p. 218), is a **parody** of his own self-importance and concern for social distinction. Pip has become imprisoned by his own snobbishness. Joe, in contrast, is a comic figure in his Sunday suit, chasing his elusive hat, but becomes truly impressive when he casts false manners aside and speaks man to man. Compare this visit to London with Magwitch's sudden arrival in Chapter 39 and Pip's terrified response to a much more formidable father figure returning from the past. As Joe says of Wopsle's acting of Hamlet with more foresight than he knows: 'if the ghost of a man's own father cannot be allowed to claim his attention, what can, Sir?' (p. 220). Pip's belated attempt to find Joe in the street at the end of the chapter recalls his better second thoughts on his departure to London in Chapter 19.

CHAPTER 28

- There are convicts on the coach when Pip returns to the local town.
- Pip discovers Pumblechook's absurd claims.

Pip quibbles with his conscience but decides to stay at the Blue Boar instead of going home to the forge. Two convicts are travelling on the coach and one of them is the stranger with the file from his childhood (Chapter 10). He overhears a conversation concerning the gift of the two pound notes and is relieved that he is not recognised. Only his adopted name of 'Handel' saves him from recognition. On his arrival, he reads a newspaper account suggesting that Pumblechook is the founder of his fortunes.

COMMENTARY

At the very moment that Pip has fresh hopes of Estella and puts a further distance between himself and the forge, his guilty childhood returns to haunt him. This is a repeated pattern (see Chapter 32 when Pip meets Estella at the coach office). The inflated newspaper gossip column concerning Pumblechook's supposed relationship to Pip is a good example of **mock-heroic** style.

CHAPTER 29

- Pip visits Miss Havisham and meets Estella again.

Pip believes that he is destined for Estella and indulges in feelings of romantic ardour. On arriving at Satis House, he discovers that

> **GLOSSARY**
>
> **Mentor** adviser to Telemachus, son of Odysseus, in Homer's *Odyssey*
>
> **Quintin Matsys** Flemish painter (1466–1530), supposedly worked as a blacksmith
>
> **VERB. SAP** Latin: *Verbum satis sapienti*, a word is enough for the wise

**CHECK
THE BOOK**

See Peter Brooks'
chapter, 'Repetition,
Repression and
Return' in his book
*Reading for the
Plot: Design and
Intention in
Narrative* (1984);
this can also be
found in Roger Sell's
'New Casebook' on
the novel. Brooks
draws attention to
the pattern of Pip's
repeated return to
the 'terror of
childhood' (p. 230)
on the marshes and
at Satis House
(Chapters 35, 43, 49,
52, 58 and 59).

Orlick is now the gatekeeper. His feelings on seeing Estella as a
fully grown woman are a mixture of pleasure and pain. He cannot
forget his childhood humiliation. Estella is flirtatious but also cold.
Walking in the garden together, she warns him that she has no heart.
Pip senses a resemblance in Estella to someone he cannot recall,
suggesting a mystery behind her identity. When they are alone, Miss
Havisham exhorts Pip to love Estella in a manner that sounds like a
curse. Jaggers arrives but gives no hint of any secrets he may have.
Pip returns to the Blue Boar to dream of Estella and ignore his duty
to visit Joe.

COMMENTARY

Pip sees himself as a hero of a romance. But his idealised vision of
rescuing Estella and giving renewed life to Satis House ill-accords
with the reality of Orlick's presence, Estella's haughty coldness,
Miss Havisham's teasing cruelty and Jaggers' secret calculation. The
mature Pip looks back with regret at his folly and neglect of his true
friend.

CHAPTER 30

- Pip is humiliated by Trabb's boy.
- He has intimate discussions with Herbert on his return to
London.

Pip suggests to Jaggers that Orlick is unsuitable for his post.
Walking through the town he meets Trabb's boy who apes his dress
and fine manners mercilessly to the delight of all. Pip takes his
revenge by ensuring his dismissal. He salves his bad conscience over
Joe by sending him a gift. Back in London, he confides his feelings
for Estella to Herbert, who warns Pip that she may not be destined
for him and is unlikely to make him happy. Herbert, in turn, tells
Pip about his secret engagement to Clara, the humble daughter of a
retired ship's purser, but, without money, they have little hope of
marriage. They console themselves by deciding to go to a play.

COMMENTARY

By this stage, our sympathy for Pip is becoming more qualified. We pity his infatuation for Estella but his treatment of those he has left behind in his social rise is mean or condescending. Consequently Trabb's boy's jeering 'don't know yah!' (p. 246) has the corrective sting of **satire** that we recognise, if the young Pip does not. His mocking behaviour is a **parody** of Pip's social pretensions, and indeed Pip does not choose to 'know' or acknowledge Joe on his visit. Herbert plays the part of the true friend, as his father did for Miss Havisham.

CHAPTER 31

- Pip and Herbert have a night at the theatre to see Waldengarver's Hamlet.

Pip and Herbert go to see Wopsle acting Hamlet. It is a farcical, undistinguished performance with much barracking from the audience. Wopsle seems impervious to his reception, however, and afterwards tells Pip of his grand plans to revive the drama.

COMMENTARY

This is an amusing set piece. However, it is not just a comic interlude providing light relief. It has links with the main action at several levels. Both Pip and Wopsle have 'great expectations' and Wopsle's are a comic variant of Pip's. As Pip has been changed into 'Handel' so Wopsle has now become the absurd 'Waldengarver'. The imagery of rottenness and decay which is associated with *Hamlet* pervades *Great Expectations*, too. While Miss Havisham is a kind of grotesque, aged Ophelia; Pip, haunted by ghosts and searching for an identity through a lost father, is something of a Hamlet, a fact he seems to recognise in his bizarre dream at the end of the chapter. He will also return (figuratively) from the 'underworld of Australia' in Chapter 39.

CONTEXT

Pip recalls that Wopsle looked as if he were 'insured in some extraordinary fire office' (p. 256). At this time buildings insured against fire had large signs on their walls to inform the appropriate fire engines which building to save.

CHAPTER 32

> GLOSSARY
>
> **quantum** sufficient sum of money
>
> **Coiner** forger

- After being taken round Newgate by Wemmick, Pip meets Estella off the London coach.

Pip receives a letter from Estella informing him of Miss Havisham's wish that he should meet her in London. Arriving early at the coach office, he comes across Wemmick who invites him to tour Newgate. Pip observes Wemmick doing business with his clients, saying farewell to a condemned man and being given 'portable property'. Afterwards, Pip is full of guilty anxiety about his tainted past, an association with crime that seems impossible to shake off. Estella's face at the coach window stirs a buried memory he cannot name.

> CONTEXT
>
> The reference to prisoners setting fire to their prisons because of the flavour of their soup (p. 260) refers to the Chatham Convict Prison Riots in 1861.

COMMENTARY

This chapter shows Wemmick going about his official business as Jaggers' agent. The professional detachment of his operations is emphasised by the use of gardening imagery that is a feature of this chapter. Outside Newgate Pip's thoughts return once more to the marshes; his concern about his criminal associations remind us of his previous contact with convicts (Chapters 1–5, 10 and 28). The mysterious 'nameless shadow' (p. 264) that stirs Pip's memory when he sees Estella recalls a similar experience he had with her in the garden of Satis House earlier (Chapter 29) and another on the coach in the next chapter. Clearly Dickens is building up a sense of mystery concerning Estella's identity.

CHAPTER 33

> GLOSSARY
>
> **Moses in the bullrushes** Moses was found in the bullrushes by Pharaoh's daughter (Exodus, 11:3–6)

- Pip and Estella take tea before he escorts her to Richmond.

Estella acts as if she and Pip are under orders. She reveals how the Pocket relations intrigue against Pip and how unhappy they made her childhood. She warns Pip against any emotional involvement with her but he feels unable to distance himself despite the pain. She is to live in London and report all her social activities to Miss Havisham. Pip returns to the domestic chaos at Hammersmith with a heavy heart.

COMMENTARY

The comic description of the tea contrasts with Estella's bitterness and Pip's unhappiness. Estella's revulsion as they pass Newgate and her distaste for Jaggers are linked with Pip's 'inexplicable feeling' (p. 269) to suggest an obscure connection.

CHAPTER 34

- Pip falls into debt and dissipation.
- Pip and Herbert attempt to take stock of their situation.
- He has news of Mrs Joe's death.

Pip's continuing idleness and lavish spending begin to affect Herbert. Along with Startop and Drummle, they seek membership of a riotous dining club called 'The Finches of the Grove'. Pip's life is aimless and Herbert cannot find employment. One evening, as they are preoccupied with their financial affairs, a letter arrives announcing Mrs Joe's death and funeral arrangements.

COMMENTARY

This is a bridging chapter that summarises a period of Pip's life, showing his gradual moral decline and guilt about Herbert, Joe and Biddy.

> **CONTEXT**
>
> Dickens makes the point of locating The Finches Club in Covent Garden, an area notorious for prostitution at the time. Thus he can suggest the nature of Pip's diversions without offending his more innocent readers.

CHAPTER 35

- A comic description of Mrs Joe's funeral.
- We have news of the forge.
- Biddy rebukes Pip.

CHECK THE BOOK

Robert Garis, *The Dickens Theatre: A Reassessment of the Novels*, Chapter 10, has a detailed discussion of this chapter.

Pip's feelings about his sister are softened by her death. He arrives at the forge to find that Trabb and Pumblechook have taken over the funeral arrangements, marginalising Joe. After the funeral Pip hears of the manner of Mrs Joe's death from Biddy, who also informs him of her plans to start a school and of Orlick's continuing attentions. Her implied criticism of Pip's neglect of Joe makes him indignant and resentful but, as he takes his leave, he knows that it is just.

COMMENTARY

This chapter shows a skilful mixture of **pathos** and **satire**. Pip's feelings about his dead sister, his own mortality, and the description of her actual internment are touchingly described. So, too, is Biddy's account of Mrs Joe's death. This contrasts with the comical description of the funeral itself which is crudely ostentatious and bogusly theatrical. The mists rising around Pip as he leaves the forge, as at the close of Chapter 19, suggest the degree of his self-deception.

CHAPTER 36

- Pip comes of age.
- He has an interview with Jaggers.
- Pip plans to help Herbert.

Pip goes to see Jaggers and is questioned over his debts. He is given five hundred pounds and told he must live on that per annum until he knows who his benefactor is. Jaggers will tell him nothing more. Pip wishes to help Herbert financially and requests help from Wemmick. Wemmick cannot discuss the matter favourably at the office and suggests that Pip come down to see him in Walworth.

COMMENTARY

Pip is convinced that Miss Havisham is his patron. Childhood memories of being put on a tombstone, the horrible death masks above Jaggers' head and his careful disassociation from any disclosure do not suggest any alternative possibility. Wemmick's grim warnings against charity in his official 'Little Britain' capacity emphasise his split personality.

CHAPTER 37

- Pip pays another visit to Walworth.
- Wemmick agrees to help Pip in his scheme.
- Pip observes the courtship of Wemmick and Miss Skiffins.

Before Wemmick's arrival, Pip enjoys a good-natured attempt at communication with the deaf, aged parent and is shown some ingenious gadgetry. After Sunday tea, Wemmick and Miss Skiffins enjoy a comically restrained courtship while the aged parent reads the newspaper. Later Wemmick arranges some money to be passed to a merchant called Clarriker so that Herbert can be employed without any knowledge of Pip's charity.

COMMENTARY

Wemmick's home is a cosy, domestic **idyll** far away from Newgate. It is an appropriate setting for Pip's one good, disinterested use of his 'expectations'. Wemmick's mechanical advances and Miss Skiffins' prudish response are pure pantomime, but also suggest the strict moral discipline required for respectability and material advancement.

CHAPTER 38

- Pip is tortured at the hands of Estella.
- Estella and Miss Havisham quarrel and she encourages Drummle's courtship.

Pip haunts Estella's house at Richmond where he is used to inflict jealousy on other suitors but feels demeaned himself. He continues

QUESTION

Discuss the significance of either Jaggers or Wemmick, both for the plot of *Great Expectations* and its themes.

to ignore her warnings, hopeful that Miss Havisham intends them to marry in the end. On a visit to Satis House, he notes Miss Havisham's increasing devotion to Estella and they quarrel when Estella says she is unable to return these feelings because her upbringing has made her heartless. After Drummle toasts Estella at a gathering of The Finches Club, Pip discovers that she has danced with Drummle on several occasions. However, Estella insists that she deceives all but him. The chapter ends with an ominous story about a Sultan crushed by a huge stone slab prepared to fall on him at his moment of greatest triumph. This, Pip tells us, was about to happen to him.

COMMENTARY

Pip deceives himself when he thinks Miss Havisham has exempted him from her revenge. All the evidence suggests otherwise. Miss Havisham herself becomes a more pitiable figure in this chapter. She, in her turn, has fallen victim to her own creation and her love, desperate in its intensity, is rejected. Estella can make no exceptions to the lessons she has been taught. The formal, rather **melodramatic**, nature of the dialogue and action at this point reflects Dickens' interest in the theatre of the time.

CHAPTER 39

• Pip's mysterious benefactor declares himself.

Pip is now twenty-three and has moved to the Temple. One stormy winter night when Herbert is away on business, a stranger arrives at Pip's door. Pip recognises him as the convict on the marshes long ago (Chapters 1–5). Pip seeks to get rid of him by a gift of two clean pound notes but the convict burns them in the fire and, with gathering horror, Pip realises who has been behind his expectations all along. The convict was transported to Australia where he made a fortune sheep-farming and decided to make Pip 'a brought-up London gentleman' (p. 321).

Pip is disgusted, disappointed and full of remorse. He can have no hope of Estella now, and he has deserted Joe on the whim of a felon. Pip reluctantly gives him shelter learning that, if recaptured, the penalty for his return is death.

COMMENTARY

This is the climax of the story and Pip's slow, drawn-out recognition that his wealth has been based on a convict's toil is handled with masterly suspense. Magwitch's interrogation of Pip as to the source of his 'expectations' is uncomfortably reminiscent of both Pumblechook and Jaggers. Even though the scene is experienced from Pip's point of view, Dickens ensures that our sympathies are evenly divided between the appalled Pip and the proud, emotional convict. The two clean pound notes are meant to be repayment for the two 'sweltering' ones (Chapter 10, p. 78) but he is not to be bought off so cheaply.

The chapter also reveals the convict's mixed motives. He considers himself Pip's 'second father' (p. 320) and wishes to show gratitude for his act of kindness but he also wants to 'own' a gentleman as an act of revenge. In this he is similar to Miss Havisham. Both Estella and Pip are partly victims and deserve our sympathy. Compare Magwitch's arrival with Joe's visit earlier (Chapter 27). His sudden, unexpected appearance echoes his first (Chapter 1) when he did indeed seem to be Pip's 'second father' risen from the grave of the first. The wet and wind of the stormy night ('like discharges of cannon' p. 313) are suggestive of that earlier scene. Pip's association with criminality begun then (Chapters 1–3) and guiltily repressed (see Chapters 10, 15, 16, 20, 28, and 32) is now finally brought to light.

CHECK THE BOOK

In *Dickens and the Invisible World*, Chapter 9, Harry Stone has a detailed commentary on this 'recognition scene', discussing the fairy-tale elements it contains.

VOLUME III

CHAPTER 40

- Pip realises the risks and dangers of Magwitch's return.
- Pip is disappointed and alarmed.
- Herbert returns.

Pip discovers a man lurking in the doorway the following morning and suspects Abel Magwitch, the convict, has been followed. He goes to Jaggers who confirms the truth of the story though not of the convict's return and denies any responsibility for Pip's belief that Miss Havisham was the source of his inheritance. Magwitch shows a childish joy in Pip's attainments but also a degree of moral delicacy. He wishes to stay and watch his gentleman take his pleasures. Although Magwitch disgusts Pip and he is tempted to run away, he is concerned for his safety. He tries to disguise Magwitch as his uncle Provis, but fears all attempts to hide his true nature are futile. Herbert returns and is sworn to secrecy.

COMMENTARY

Magwitch's concern not to be 'low' (p. 332) suggests someone more complex than Pip's lurid portrait at this stage. His crude eating habits are an exaggerated version of Pip's own when he first came to London (Chapter 22). Pip watches him with very different feelings from those long ago on the marshes (Chapter 3). Like Joe, all attempts to change his dress cannot disguise his true nature and again like Joe he takes pleasure in hearing Pip read languages he cannot master himself. Jaggers' refusal to implicate himself in Pip's problems is harsh, but to be expected.

GLOSSARY

Botany Bay where transported convicts disembarked in Australia

shorts knee breeches

Calendar the *Newgate Calendar* (1771). Stories of notorious criminals

---

CONTEXT

'the imaginary student' is the hero of Mary Shelley's *Frankenstein* (1818) The reference to *Frankenstein* is complex and particularly apt. Pip is both Frankenstein and his creature; he is frightened of Magwitch as a monster but he has been 'made' by Magwitch into something of a monster himself.

CHAPTER 41

- Pip confides in Herbert.

Herbert learns the truth of Pip's situation and when Magwitch leaves for his night's lodgings, they discuss the future. Pip says that he cannot accept Magwitch's patronage. Fearful of what he might do if he knew this, they plan to take him to safety abroad before Pip can free himself from his obligation. When Magwitch returns in the morning eager to start spending money, they ask him about his past.

COMMENTARY

Already Pip feels responsible for his unwelcome benefactor. The emphasis in this chapter is on the warm friendship between Pip and Herbert as they plan what is best to do, and the fact that Pip, now an impoverished gentleman, has no profession or trade with which to make his independent way in the world.

CHAPTER 42

- Magwitch tells his story.

Magwitch tells of his harsh, poverty-stricken upbringing that led, inevitably, to early crime and punishment by an indifferent or hostile society. He tells also of his involvement with Compeyson, the fellow convict with whom Pip saw him struggle on the marshes long ago (Chapter 5). Compeyson was a cruel, sophisticated villain with good social connections and Magwitch became his partner. An earlier associate, Arthur, died of drink, driven mad with guilt over a deed in the past involving money and a rich lady. Magwitch became increasingly ensnared in Compeyson's criminal activities and when they were brought to trial, it was Magwitch who got the harsher sentence because he looked like a villain and had a previous record, while Compeyson was a gentleman. Driven by a need for revenge, Magwitch fought with Compeyson on the marshes to foil his

GLOSSARY

Summun Magwitch's version of 'someone'

taturs potatoes

Traveller's Rest a shelter used by tramps

the horrors delirium caused by alcoholism

Bridewells and Lock-ups names for prisons

CONTEXT

When he says
'they measured my
head' (p. 346)
Magwitch is
referring to
phrenology, a
popular pseudo-
science in the
nineteenth
century. There was
a belief that the
shape of the skull
determined the
character, and that
there were certain
'criminal types'.

escape, even though it ensured his own recapture. He doesn't know
what happened to Compeyson. When he finishes his tale, Herbert
secretly informs Pip that Miss Havisham's brother was called
Arthur, and Compeyson was the name of her lover.

COMMENTARY

Like Herbert's story of Miss Havisham (Chapter 22), Magwitch
provides essential information for the plot by narrating events that
have happened in the distant past and that Pip could not have given
the reader himself. Despite his lack of education, Magwitch is an
effective narrator and his tale is important for the theme of the novel
as well as the plot. It casts light on social injustice and why
Magwitch needs to make and 'own' a gentleman as recompense for
his past ill treatment and being 'made' into a criminal. As an orphan,
his memories of his early childhood are very similar to Pip's, which
partly explains his fondness for the boy and how, in time, the older
Pip will come to reciprocate these feelings. Herbert's revelation
links the Magwitch story with that of Miss Havisham. Further
points of interest for the reader are the possible whereabouts of
Compeyson and the teasing scrap of information that Magwitch had
a wife, although nothing is made of that now.

CHAPTER 43

- Pip decides to see Miss Havisham and Estella before going
  abroad.
- Drummle is staying at the Blue Boar.

Pip realises that Magwitch is in danger if Compeyson is alive and
knows of his return. Estella is not at Richmond so Pip goes down to
Satis House. He discovers Drummle is staying at the Blue Boar and
clearly playing court to Estella. The rivals try to ignore one another
and then compete over the fireplace in a ridiculous manner.
Drummle goads Pip with his successful courtship of Estella and the
knowledge of Pip's humble origins. As Drummle leaves for his ride,
Pip thinks that he spots Orlick.

COMMENTARY

As he prepares to say his farewells at Satis House, Pip sees no possible connection between the proud and beautiful Estella and the outcast convict Magwitch, but more revelations are in store. A possible relationship between Drummle and the shadowy Orlick strikes an ominous note with which to end the chapter.

CHAPTER 44

- Pip asks a favour of Miss Havisham and declares his love to Estella.
- Estella is engaged to Drummle.
- Pip returns to London.

Miss Havisham confirms that she used Pip's good fortune to torture her relatives and the fact that Jaggers acted for both her and Pip's patron was mere coincidence: 'You made your own snares. *I* never made them' (p. 360). Pip tells her not to judge Matthew or Herbert Pocket like the others and requests that she complete the financial help he has given, secretly, to Herbert because now he will be unable to do so himself. He tells Estella he will always love her because she is part of him, for better or worse. She does not understand his emotional appeal and informs him of her imminent marriage to Drummle. Pip is distraught and even Miss Havisham shows some sign of remorse as he leaves in despair. On his return to London, he finds a note from Wemmick saying 'Don't go home' (p. 334).

COMMENTARY

Estella's news marks the final collapse of all Pip's 'expectations'. She calls him 'a visionary boy' (p. 364) and his investment in an idealised vision of her as a completion of his own identity, although moving, suggests an adolescent infatuation that is doomed to failure. It is a measure of his gathering moral strength and growing maturity, however, that even at this time he can think of Herbert before himself. We may find Miss Havisham's judgement on Pip's credulity

CHECK THE BOOK
Steven Connor discusses Pip's obsessive conjugation of 'Don't go home' during his bad night as an indication of how he is caught up and 'conjugated' by an impersonal system over which he has no control. See his *Charles Dickens* (1985).

rather harsh. It is true that there were some ambiguous signs to the contrary if he had chosen to focus on them, but the circumstantial evidence that pointed to Miss Havisham as being his benefactor was very strong. Others, beside Pip, were taken in. Wemmick's note makes a dramatic, 'cliff-hanging' conclusion to this weekly part.

GLOSSARY

Hummums ˙ the odd name derives from Turkish Baths

Argus in Greek mythology, Argus had a hundred eyes

CHAPTER 45

- Pip spends a bad night at the Hummums Hotel.
- Wemmick has news of Compeyson, and Magwitch is removed to Mill Pond Bank.

Pip spends an anxious night in a run-down hotel before seeing Wemmick at Walworth. Compeyson is in London and Pip's rooms are being watched. Herbert has managed to hide Magwitch away in the house by the river where his fiancée, Clara Barley (Chapter 30), lives with her father. Pip spends the day at Walworth before leaving after dark.

COMMENTARY

Note how suspenseful developments in the narrative are interspersed with comic writing on Pip's hotel bedroom and breakfast at Walworth.

GLOSSARY

Double Gloucester a famous English cheese

to 'shoot' the bridge to steer through the narrow arches

CHAPTER 46

- We learn of the domestic arrangements at Mill Pond Bank.
- Pip and Herbert make preparations for Magwitch's escape.

Pip finds the house by the docks. Clara Barley's father, Bill Barley, is a drunken, domestic tyrant who bullies his daughter from his bed, roaring and knocking on the floor. Pip envies Herbert and Clara their happiness, comparing their quiet contentment with his painful parting from Estella. He believes Magwitch has become more gentle and leaves him with anxious regret. Along with Herbert, he starts to row regularly on the river to avoid suspicion and in readiness for boarding a ship. A drawn blind on Magwitch's window is a sign that all is well.

Commentary

The relationship between Pip and Magwitch has begun to change. Pip has become more purposeful, and thinks less about himself. Compare Bill Barley's treatment of his daughter with Wemmick's treatment of the aged parent.

Chapter 47

- There is a sinister figure in the audience at Wopsle's pantomime.

Some weeks pass as Pip waits for a sign from Wemmick to carry out the escape plan. He is in debt but will not use Magwitch's money. Wopsle's acting career has not been successful and one evening Pip watches his performance in an absurd pantomime. However, Wopsle spends most of his time on stage watching Pip. Afterwards he accosts Pip, recounts the events on the marshes long ago, and informs him that he is sure one of the convicts was sitting behind him during the play. Pip realises it must be Compeyson. He and Herbert increase their vigilance.

Commentary

Once again we have an absurd, **farcical** account of one of Wopsle's performances (see Chapters 15, 18 and 31). But the real drama takes place off stage. Pip, while watching, is being watched. Wopsle's retelling of the fateful day on the marshes (Chapter 5) is far more dramatic than any of his more theatrical performances. Note how his declining fortunes **parody** Pip's. There is some irony in the fact that although he is no longer playing Hamlet, Wopsle like Hamlet has now seen a memorable 'ghost' from the past.

GLOSSARY

swab a term of abuse used by sailors

 QUESTION

Discuss Wopsle's role in *Great Expectations*. Would the loss of this character diminish the overall effect of this novel?

GLOSSARY

put in all the salt and pepper did all the important work

over the broomstick marriage in the gipsy way

CHAPTER 48

- Pip has dinner with Jaggers and Wemmick.
- There are revelations concerning the housekeeper.

Pip meets Jaggers by chance and dines with him and Wemmick. He learns that Miss Havisham wishes to see him and he is pained to hear of Estella's marriage. Jaggers insists that Drummle will either 'beat or cringe' (p. 390). When Molly, the housekeeper (Chapter 26), is summonsed, a knitting action of her hands finally confirms a vague intimation that Pip has had for some time (see Chapters 29, 32 and 33). Estella is Molly's daughter. Walking home, Wemmick tells how Jaggers managed to get her acquitted of a murder against all the odds. She had been married to a tramp and was charged with strangling another woman in a jealous rage. There were rumours that she had murdered her child, a little girl.

COMMENTARY

More mysteries are coming to light and another link between the criminal world and Satis House is established. Estella's mother is a murderess. But who is Estella's father and how did she come to be in Miss Havisham's care? Jaggers' harsh prediction of Estella's marriage seems typically cynical, but there is much beating and cringing generally in this novel (see **Themes: Beating and cringing**).

CHAPTER 49

- Pip has a final meeting with Miss Havisham.
- Miss Havisham repents and there is a fatal accident.

Miss Havisham gives Pip the nine hundred pounds he needs to ensure secretly Herbert's partnership with Clarriker, but although she offers, he requests nothing for himself. Dramatically she begs for forgiveness which Pip freely gives. His own suffering has given him understanding of others' pain. Miss Havisham meant well when Estella came to live with her at first but gradually her need for revenge became too strong for her and she turned Estella's heart to ice. She can tell Pip nothing of Estella's parentage. As a young child, Estella was brought to Satis House by Jaggers and she believed her to be an orphan. Pip takes a final walk in the ruined garden before his departure and believes, once again (Chapter 8), that he sees Miss Havisham hanging from a beam. Acting on impulse, he returns to the house to see Miss Havisham accidentally set fire to her bridal dress. Wrapping her in the remnants of her great tablecloth, he burns his own hand badly. She is laid on the dining table as she had prophesied (Chapter 11). As Pip leaves, she is still begging forgiveness.

COMMENTARY

Pip's moral regeneration continues. He is able to forgive Miss Havisham for the wrong she has done him because he knows he needs forgiveness himself. He understands her real crime was willed isolation from life and he acts bravely in saving her. Her repentance and the accident are described with great theatrical drama and the burning of the wedding clothes and dining cloth are appropriate **symbolically**. Miss Havisham has repented, but the trappings of her old, morbid existence have destroyed her. Pip's burnt hand also carries symbolic meaning. It is part of his punishment for severing old bonds with the forge and becoming ensnared in Miss Havisham's perverted schemes.

 QUESTION

Discuss the symbolic importance of fire in *Great Expectations*.

CHAPTER 50

- Pip learns from Herbert that Estella is Magwitch's child.

Back in London, Pip is nursed by Herbert. Attending to his burns, Herbert tells him what he has learned from Magwitch about his wife. It becomes clear that this is the same woman who is now Jaggers' housekeeper. Magwitch first knew of Jaggers through the trial and hid away for fear of incriminating her still further. He

QUESTION

Discuss how Dickens reveals the hidden connections between respectability and crime in *Great Expectations*.

never saw her again. They had a child, a little girl, and Magwitch assumes, because of his wife's jealous threats, that she was murdered too. Compeyson knew all this and used the information to get Magwitch still further into his power. All this happened three or four years before the events on the marshes (Chapters 1–5) and the young Pip recalled tender feelings of Magwitch's own lost daughter, who was about Pip's age.

COMMENTARY

The connection between the churchyard on the marshes, Jaggers' criminal world and Satis House is now complete. Estella, who seemed so ideal and remote, a pure and distant star, is revealed to be the daughter of a convict and a murderess. Both Pip and Estella are tainted with crime.

CHAPTER 51

- There are further revelations in Jaggers' office.

Pip goes to Little Britain to inform Jaggers of Miss Havisham's accident and give him her instructions for Herbert's money. Both Jaggers and Wemmick are disappointed that Pip has nothing for himself. As Wemmick states emphatically, 'Every man's business in portable property' (p. 409). Even Jaggers is surprised by Pip's information about Estella's father and that Wemmick has The Aged at home. After Pip's impassioned plea, he finally tells all that he knows, 'admitting nothing' (p. 412). He defended Molly at her trial on the understanding that she would give up her concealed child if she were freed. He knew Miss Havisham wished to adopt a little girl and that the father was in hiding and believed his daughter dead. Jaggers has seen many innocent young children born into a life of crime and hardship; he wished to save at least one from inevitable destruction. After the trial Estella went to Miss Havisham and Molly sought protection from Jaggers as his housekeeper. All agree that this new information is best left secret from those concerned. Jaggers and Wemmick seem rather uncomfortable with the insights each now has of the other's humanity until the arrival of Mike (Chapter 20) allows them to be cheerfully brutal.

COMMENTARY

Pip's new moral strength is shown in his successful appeal to Jaggers. He has managed to unearth information that even Jaggers, the master of secrets, does not know. Jaggers completes the missing details in a story begun by Wemmick (Chapter 48), continued by Miss Havisham (Chapter 49) and, via Herbert, Magwitch (Chapter 50). Pip's persistence has finally revealed the truth and he has mastered the plot rather than being controlled by the plots of others. For once, too, humanity and openness are shown in Jaggers' office. But, although this has its humorous side, it is not without risks. Pip almost fears that his revelation of the aged parent may cost Wemmick his job and he is careful not to implicate him in his discoveries to Jaggers. Both Jaggers and Wemmick are relieved to return to their professional roles.

CHECK THE BOOK

Harry Stone discusses Orlick's association with the devil in *Dickens and the Invisible World*, Chapter 9.

CHAPTER 52

- Pip performs one good act with his expectations.
- He makes preparations for Magwitch's escape.
- Pip receives a mysterious letter.

Pip has the satisfaction of securing Herbert's partnership with Clarriker's firm. Herbert is likely to be sent abroad quite soon. One Monday in March, Wemmick writes urging them to get Magwitch away without delay and careful plans are finalised to take him from his hiding place on Wednesday, row down river and board the Hamburg steamer from a quiet spot. Because of his injuries, Pip will steer and Startop will help row the boat. Pip will take his chance with Magwitch. Later that day, he receives a mysterious letter telling him to go to the sluicehouse by the lime kiln on the marshes if he would hear more of his uncle Provis, and to keep the matter secret. In haste and without thought of precautions, Pip catches the afternoon coach, saying he has gone to Satis House to inquire after Miss Havisham. After a brief call there, he learns at a local inn that Pumblechook is still claiming to be his earliest benefactor and complaining of his ingratitude. Realising that he has lost the letter and thinking sadly of Joe, Pip sets off for the marshes.

COMMENTARY

Old mysteries have been dispelled but a new one now appears. Once more Pip has been drawn to the marsh.

CHAPTER 53

- Pip has a confrontation with Orlick at the sluicehouse.
- Pip is rescued just in time.

CHECK THE FILM

David Lean's film (and indeed most other film versions) cut Orlick and his violent plots. In Lean's film, Mrs Joe simply dies and Biddy replaces her in the household, a clear departure from the text.

Pip crosses the marshes in the dark. He finds the abandoned sluicehouse where he is surprised and bound by Orlick. Orlick intends to take his revenge on Pip for the loss of his job at Satis House and spoiling all his hopes with Biddy. He intends to kill him with a heavy stone hammer and burn his body in the lime kiln. Drinking heavily, he confesses to the assault on Mrs Joe (Chapter 15) and it was he who was lurking on the stairs when Magwitch first arrived back in London (Chapter 40). Orlick now works for Compeyson. Pip, sadly thinking how others will remember him, expects to die and fears for Magwitch's safety but Herbert and Startop, led by Trabb's boy, arrive just in time. Herbert has found the letter in Pip's apartment and suspected a plot. Orlick flees and they decide not to pursue him until after Magwitch's escape. Pip returns to London, feverish and sick with the pain from his burnt arm but when he awakes on Wednesday morning he is full of fresh hope.

COMMENTARY

Orlick has dogged Pip throughout his life (Chapters 15, 16, 17, 29, 35, 40 and 43) and it seems that this final, melodramatic confrontation is a necessary purging of his darker self. Pip felt obscurely guilty for his sister's injuries (Chapter 16) and Orlick claims that he was indeed responsible. Orlick's torture brings out Pip's genuine repentance, finer feelings and concern for others. Having survived the experience, Pip seems cleansed of his guilt. This is **symbolised** by the bright morning weather that ends this chapter.

CHAPTER 54

- The escape attempt is unsuccessful.
- Compeyson is drowned and Magwitch badly hurt.
- Pip has lost his expectations.

Pip, Herbert and Startop pause to pick up Magwitch as they row through the busy port of London and beyond Gravesend into the remoter reaches of the estuary. Magwitch shows great gratitude to Pip and a calm acceptance of his destiny. As darkness falls they find a lonely inn in which to stay for the night and learn of a four-oared galley that has been lurking in the area. Pip wakes in the night to see two men inspecting their boat. In the morning Pip and Magwitch walk together before they all row out into the track of the approaching Hamburg steamer. They are intercepted by the galley which is a police launch. Magwitch unmasks a cloaked figure as Compeyson and there is a struggle. The steamer runs down Pip's boat, Compeyson is drowned and Magwitch is severely injured in his head and chest. Pip accompanies the rearrested convict to London. Magwitch is consoled by the thought that Pip is now a gentleman but Pip knows that he has lost all hope of riches now.

COMMENTARY

This is a chapter of sustained narrative excitement and mounting tension that reaches a climax in the struggle between Magwitch and Compeyson. The desolate estuary is reminiscent of the marshes of Pip's childhood, and the struggle is a repetition of the one in the muddy ditch all those years ago (Chapter 5). It represents the final victory of the reformed convict, *Abel* Magwitch over his irredeemably wicked adversary, who carries a mark on his face like

GLOSSARY

coal-whippers men who loaded or unloaded coal barges

ballast-lighters barges carrying ballast for sailing ships

As the tide made as the tide flowed more strongly

thowels wooden pegs to hold the oars

Jack odd job man

CONTEXT

Dickens drew up a table of Thames tides to check the plausibility of his story. According to John Forster, his first biographer, he hired a steamer for the day from Blackwall to Southend, 'to make himself sure of the actual course of a boat in such circumstances'.

Cain, the first murderer (see the Bible story, Genesis, 4:8–15). Once again Magwitch is led away in chains but we, like Pip, understand his situation better and can make a more informed moral judgement. The river, as Magwitch sees, marks the flow of life and destiny. Pip is now able to see in Magwitch, 'a much better man than I had been to Joe' (p. 446). He will stand by him to the end despite the loss of his wealth. Note the wonderful characterisation of the 'Jack' at the inn, a vivid sketch in this chapter only.

GLOSSARY

the red book gives the names and addresses of the aristocracy

Hymen the classical goddess of marriage

Provided by contract paid in advance

CHAPTER 55

- Herbert is to go abroad.
- Wemmick has a surprise wedding.

Magwitch's trial is delayed until he can be identified. Jaggers tells Pip that the verdict is a forgone conclusion. Herbert is to start a new business venture for Clarriker in Egypt. He hopes that Clara will soon be free to marry him and begs Pip to join them as clerk in the new branch with prospects of rapid promotion. Pip agrees to consider it soon. Wemmick explains that he thought Compeyson was away from London because of conversations he had overheard, but he has been deliberately misled. Like Jaggers, he is disappointed at the 'sacrifice of so much portable property' (p. 451). He asks Pip to call for him on the following Monday. This turns out to be for the occasion of Wemmick's marriage to Miss Skiffins. Although everything is carefully planned, Wemmick insists on pretending that it is all casual and spontaneous. He asks Pip to tell Jaggers nothing of this. It is Walworth not Little Britain business.

COMMENTARY

Even at this dark, late stage in Pip's fortunes, Dickens manages to insert a humorous episode. Wemmick's domestic happiness is an appropriate reward for his kindness to Pip. He remains a divided man to the last. Herbert's promotion and prospect of marrying a kind, unsnobbish girl also emphasise Pip's growing isolation.

CHAPTER 56

- A description of the sickness, trial and conviction of Magwitch.
- Magwitch learns of his daughter on his death-bed.

As Magwitch lies sick in the prison hospital, Pip tries vainly to petition for his pardon. He attends on Magwitch daily in prison and in court. On the final day of the Sessions when the death sentence is passed on thirty-two people together, Magwitch responds to the judge with dignity and resignation. He dies before the sentence can be carried out but Pip is able to tell him in his last moments that his daughter still lives, is a grand lady and that he loves her.

COMMENTARY

Marriage and thoughts of marriage in the last chapter are followed by a death in this. As with the loss of his fortune, Pip protects Magwitch from the full truth of his daughter. Estella may have become a lady but, as he has become a gentleman, only at a cost. He may love her, but that love is now hopeless. The trial scene, with the April sunlight linking both judge and condemned, shows the serious side of Dickens' Christian morality and social criticism. All those in the courtroom, fashionable observers and hopeless wretches alike, will face a verdict on their lives at the last judgement. The reference to the parable of the publican and the Pharisee with which the chapter ends, suggests that Magwitch is a sincere, humble penitent, while Pip recognises that for much of the book, he has acted like the proud Pharisee.

CONTEXT

Pip's reference to 'the two men, who went up into the Temple to pray' (p. 460) comes from Luke, 18:10–14. The famous parable concerns two men who went into the temple to pray, one a publican and the other a Pharisee who was a member of a strict Jewish sect. The Pharisee thanked God that he was not 'as other men are' because of his strict observance of religious rules while the publican simply 'smote on his breast saying "God be merciful to me a sinner"'. Because of this parable, being a Pharisee has become synonymous with being a self-righteous religious hypocrite. Pip substitutes 'to him, a sinner' for the original 'to me, a sinner' and some critics have thought that this misquotation suggests that his moral conversation is far from complete.

CHAPTER 57

- Pip faces imprisonment for debt and becomes ill.
- Joe nurses him back to health and pays his creditors.

Pip is harassed by debt collectors and falls dangerously ill. When he

GLOSSARY
coddleshell Joe's attempt at 'codicil', an addition to a will

CONTEXT
The debt-collector talks about his 'very nice house' (p. 462). Bailiffs could take debtors to 'sponging houses' where they stayed until their creditors were paid off.

recovers from his feverish delirium, he finds that Joe has come to take care of him. Pip is full of intense gratitude and, in his weakened state, he rediscovers his old childish dependency on Joe. Biddy has taught Joe to write and informs her of the good news before telling Pip about events back home. Miss Havisham has died, giving her Pocket relatives appropriately derisory legacies, except Matthew who has four thousand pounds on Pip's recommendation. Orlick has been jailed for breaking into Pumblechook's house and stealing from him after tying him up and stuffing his mouth full of flowers. Joe gives his reasons for failing to protect Pip as a child and, through Biddy's efforts, he understands why Pip didn't confide in him about the convict and the file. But as Pip's strength returns, so the distance between them widens. One morning, Pip wakens to find Joe gone and that his debts have been paid. He resolves to return to the forge and ask Biddy to marry him.

COMMENTARY

The reconciliation of Joe and Pip is one of Christian compassion and forgiveness. Pip's illness is one more aspect of the purgatorial suffering that will cleanse him of the taints of 'expectations' and allow him to see clearly again as he did as a child. In Chapter 7, Pip 'had a new consciousness that I was looking up to Joe in my heart' (p. 50) and now, once more, he values Joe at his true worth: 'God bless this gentle Christian man' (p. 463): Pip's careful phrasing makes the moral point. One cannot be a true gentleman unless one is truly gentle. The matter of Pip's guilty secret and his failure of trust in Joe (see Chapter 6) are finally addressed (pp. 468–9). However, Dickens is also sombre and realistic. The social distance between the two cannot be bridged once Pip has recovered. Pip still has lessons to learn about the irrevocable consequences of social advancement, as his day-dreams about Biddy reveal. Joe's information about Miss Havisham, Orlick and Pumblechook is given in typically comic style and ties up a few more loose ends with some appropriate rewards and punishments. There is still some fun at Joe's expense as he sits down to write his letter to Biddy but this is double-edged for it is Biddy, not Pip, who has taught Joe to read and write.

CHAPTER 58

- Pip returns to the forge to find it is Joe and Biddy's wedding day.

Pip finds his reception at the Blue Boar is not as it was when he had 'expectations'. Going out early he discovers that Satis House is up for sale and is to be pulled down. At breakfast he is patronised by the hypocritical Pumblechook who claims much sorrow at his fall. Pip walks to the forge in bright June weather full of good resolve to settle down only to find that Biddy has married Joe. After the first shock, Pip is relieved that he did not confide his intention to Joe before he left town. He asks and receives their forgiveness before telling them of his intention to go abroad and pay off his debts. He requests that they accompany him to the village finger post before they say their goodbyes. We learn that Pip did join Herbert in business abroad and that after a few months, the tyrannical Bill Barley's death allowed Herbert to marry his beloved Clara. Pip lived happily with them both. The firm flourished in a modest way and eventually Pip was made a partner.

COMMENTARY

Pumblechook remains irrepressible to the end. His fake lamentations contrast with Joe's true friendship. Pip's shock at Biddy's marriage shows that his painful education is still unfinished, although his final parting from Joe and Biddy contrasts strongly with his first (Chapter 19). His one, unselfish act will provide his social salvation through hard work but emotionally he is still crippled by his experiences. Marriages take place around him, but he remains a bachelor, dependent emotionally on Herbert and Clara. In his notes for the novel, Dickens wrote of Pip's generosity to Herbert: 'The one good thing he did in his prosperity, the only thing that endures and bears good fruit.'

CONTEXT

By Victorian times Britain had a large and growing empire. Note how Dickens uses the British colonies as a means of enabling plot and solving problems of plot. New South Wales is a place of punishment that allows Magwitch to amass a big fortune in secret. The Levant is a convenient and vaguely benign space also outside the plot that allows Herbert and Pip to retain their status and moderate affluence as gentlemen without Dickens having to ask the kind of questions about wealth, class and exploitation that so preoccupy him in the main story.

CHAPTER 59

• Aftermath. Pip returns and has a final meeting with Estella.

When an older Pip returns to the forge after an eleven year absence, he finds a little Pip, Joe and Biddy's child, in his place by the fireside. He takes him to the churchyard and places him on his parents' tombstone, as he was once placed long ago (Chapter 1). Biddy tells him he should marry and have children of his own but he doesn't think it likely. Biddy asks if he still thinks of Estella and he replies that his poor dream is over. However, he decides to visit the site of the old house for her sake. He knows that Drummle treated her badly before being killed by a horse two years ago. Satis House has gone, but the garden remains. Walking alone in the early winter evening mist, he sees a ghostly figure. It is Estella. She, too, has come to bid a last farewell before the land is built on. She is much changed, her heart softened by her suffering. She can better understand Pip's feelings now. They agree to remain friends apart, but as the moon rises and the mists disperse, Pip can see 'the shadow of no parting from her' (p. 484).

COMMENTARY

Pip returns once more to the scenes of his childhood. Going to the churchyard with young Pip is a kind of commemoration. The older Pip has begun to give form and significance to his own life and he seems to see in Joe and Biddy's children the hope of a better future denied to him and Estella. In this final chapter, Dickens attempts to bring these damaged children of the previous generation together into some kind of relationship, but the result is, at best, ambiguous. Estella says that they will 'continue friends apart' (p. 484). Will they marry or does the shadow warn of subsequent partings? By phrasing the last sentence in this way, Dickens, no doubt, intends us to remain uncertain of the future (see **Note on the text** and **Narrative techniques; Ambiguously ever after**).

CHECK THE FILM

The ending of the Lean version is very different. Indeed film versions generally evade the ambiguous original ending preferring the happy end of a love story. In Lean's 1946 film Estella remains unmarried because Drummle rejected her on learning of her parentage. Pip discovers her indoors, a still substantial Satis House taking over the role of Miss Havisham. Like the 'young Knight of romance' (Chapter 10, p. 231) he does indeed fulfil the dream scenario of his fantasy world and rescue the princess from her prison. He rips down the tattered curtains bringing daylight into the dingy room, and the young couple run out into the sunlight together. Although emotionally satisfying, this would seem to be a complete perversion of Dickens' original intention.

EXTENDED COMMENTARIES

TEXT 1   (PAGES 26–7)

Joe's station and influence were something feebler (if possible) when there was company, than when there was none. But he always aided and comforted me when he could, in some way of his own, and he always did so at dinner-time by giving me gravy, if there were any. There being plenty of gravy to-day, Joe spooned into my plate, at this point, about half a pint.

A little later on in the dinner, Mr Wopsle reviewed the sermon with some severity, and intimated – in the usual hypothetical case of the Church being 'thrown open' – what kind of sermon *he* would have given them. After favouring them with some heads on that discourse, he remarked that he considered the subject of the day's homily, ill chosen; which was less excusable, he added, when there were so many subjects 'going about.'

'True again,' said Uncle Pumblechook. 'You've hit it sir! Plenty of subjects going about, for them that knows how to put salt upon their tails. That's what's wanted. A man needn't go far to find a subject, if he's ready with his salt-box.' Mr Pumblechook added, after a short interval of refection, 'Look at Pork alone. There's a subject! If you want a subject, look at Pork!'

'True, sir. Many a moral for the young,' returned Mr Wopsle; and I knew he was going to lug me in, before he said it; 'might be deduced from that text.'

('You listen to this,' said my sister to me, in a severe parenthesis.)

Joe gave me some more gravy.

'Swine,' pursued Mr Wopsle, in his deepest voice, and pointing his fork at my blushes, as if he were mentioning my Christian name; 'Swine were the companions of the prodigal. The gluttony of Swine is put before us, as an example to the young.' (I thought this pretty well in him who had been praising up the pork for being so plump and juicy.) 'What is detestable in a pig, is more detestable in a boy.'

'Or girl,' suggested Mr Hubble.

CONTEXT

In a discarded ending, Dickens had the two meet briefly in a busy London street and go their separate ways, but was persuaded to change it by another novelist, Bulwer-Lytton. Some readers have felt that Dickens' first intention was the best because it was more plausible and in keeping with the prevailing mood.

CHECK THE BOOK

Barbara Hardy has an interesting chapter on the significance of food and eating in the novel in her book *The Moral Art of Dickens: Essays* (1970).

'Of course, or girl, Mr Hubble,' assented Mr Wopsle, rather irritably, 'but there is no girl present.'

'Besides,' said Mr Pumblechook, turning sharp on me, 'think what you've got to be grateful for. If you'd been born a Squeaker –'

'He *was*, if ever a child was,' said my sister, most emphatically.

Joe gave me some more gravy.

'Well, but I mean a four-footed Squeaker,' said Mr Pumblechook. 'If you had been born such, would you have been here now? Not you –'

'Unless in that form,' said Mr Wopsle, nodding towards the dish.

'But I don't mean in that form, sir,' returned Mr Pumblechook, who had an objection to being interrupted; 'I mean, enjoying himself with his elders and betters, and improving himself with their conversation, and rolling in the lap of luxury. Would he have been doing that? No, he wouldn't. And what would have been your destination?' turning on me again. 'You would have been disposed of for so many shillings according to the market price of the article, and Dunstable the butcher would have come up to you as you lay in the straw, and he would have whipped you under his left arm, and with his right he would have tucked up his frock to get a penknife from out of his waistcoat-pocket, and he would have shed your blood and had your life. No bringing up by hand then. Not a bit of it!'

Joe offered me more gravy, which I was afraid to take.

This passage is taken from Chapter 4 and is part of the Christmas dinner at the forge. It occurs just after Pip's theft of the brandy and pork pie. In the next chapter, he will join the hunt and witness the recapture of the convict. It is one of a number of scenes that show people eating (see **Imagery and symbolism**). Having fed the convict and expressed his pleasure that he enjoyed his meal, Pip is enduring a very unpleasant meal himself. Later, in Chapter 8, he is reduced to tears by Estella when she gives him food 'like a dog in disgrace' (p. 62) and he is treated no better here. Christmas should be a time for Christian charity and happiness for children, but there is only hypocrisy and victimisation at Mrs Joe's table. 'Swine' is Pip's

'Christian' name. We can understand why he should be 'morally timid and very sensitive' (Chapter 8, p. 63).

Pip is telling his story with some detachment here. We are aware of a distance between the older Pip and his younger self. The passage opens with his affectionate commentary on Joe's ineffectual attempts to comfort him with gravy. The older narrator has a sophisticated vocabulary, using words like 'intimated', 'parenthesis' and 'homily'. When he reports directly from the conversation of the others, he does so in a disdainful, mocking way. His language is rather polished and abstract, but he stresses the inappropriately literal quality of theirs in phrases like 'thrown open' and 'going about'. However, Pip as narrator yields increasingly to Pip the reporter. After the first two paragraphs, apart from brief asides, the passage is given over to the speech of others, especially Wopsle and Pumblechook who seek to dominate the conversation.

Pumblechook's speech in the third paragraph is typically assertive with plenty of short sentences. Pip is being ironical when he suggests that Pumblechook is capable of reflection; he is obviously keen to carry on hearing the sound of his own voice. His inaccurate grammar in the phrase 'them that knows' suggests he is not very educated. In a rather absurd way, he takes the figurative idea of subjects of sermons 'going about' quite literally by using the old wife's tale that one can catch a chicken by putting salt on its tail. By association, the subject he catches with his salt-box is not chicken but pork.

This gives Wopsle his cue to launch into a theatrical mock sermon directed at Pip. 'Pointing his fork at my blushes' is a comic example of **metonymy**; little Pip is reduced to a symptom of his embarrassment. This is not the only time that Pip is given a role in the narratives of others. In Chapter 15, Wopsle casts him in a dramatic reading as George Barnwell, the murderer, while Pumblechook looks on saying, 'Take warning boy, take warning!' (p. 117). In this case, Pip is to be the Prodigal Son in the New Testament parable (Luke 15:11–32). Wopsle's sententious rhetoric is deflated by Pip's witty asides but actually carries a serious point. Pip has just stolen from his family for a convict, and might well see

www. **CHECK THE NET**
For information about Lillo's play, *George Barnwell*, and its significance for Pip's story see **http://www..umd. umich.edu/casl/ hum/eng/classes/ 434/geweb/** under 'Theatres and Fairs'.

CONTEXT

When he says 'Swine were the companions of the prodigal' (p. 27), Wopsle is referring to the parable of the Prodigal Son (Luke 15:32). The Prodigal Son became a swineherd. Pip's own story is a variant of this parable, one that would have been well known to Dickens' original readers.

himself as an outcast. It is worth noting, however, that Wopsle's version of the story is not very accurate: the Prodigal is starving rather than gluttonous and would 'fain have filled his belly with the husks that the swine did eat' (Luke, 15:16). Moreover, he chooses to concentrate on the Prodigal's exile rather than the ultimate reconciliation with the father, which more accurately prefigures Pip's story.

The conversation takes an even nastier turn when Pumblechook regains the initiative. Pip is transformed into a pig and his death at the hands of Dunstable, the butcher, is detailed with horrible relish in a series of simple coordinated sentences leading up to a grand climax. Pip is to be murdered and eaten. Slaughtered rather than brought-up 'by hand'. Again, this picks up the cannibalistic imagery that is a feature of earlier chapters. Magwitch has threatened to cut his throat, eat his cheeks, and 'have (his) heart and liver out' (Chapter 1, p. 5). The visitors at the forge seem no less predatory than he is. It is a comic idea that Pip is 'improving himself' with the conversation of his betters, or 'rolling in the lap of luxury'. His 'betters' seem as intent on feasting on him as they are on the 'plump and juicy' pork. In his sister's eyes, he has always been 'a Squeaker' on two legs, if not on four.

Actually, Pumblechook's dreadful prophesy nearly comes true at the end of the book. Orlick ambushes Pip at the sluicehouse, calls him 'wolf' and announces 'I'm a going to have your life' (Chapter 53, p. 425), just as he felled his sister, 'like a bullock' (p. 428). So imaginary terrors can become real ones, and people can be treated like animals.

Young Pip and Joe remain silent throughout. The speech of the others is punctuated by quiet servings of gravy but, by the end of the passage, no amount can soothe Pip's fears.

He feels more akin to the convict outside on the marsh and imagines the soldiers are coming for him at the end of the chapter. In the next, as Joe repairs the manacles, he thinks 'what terrible good sauce for a dinner my fugitive friend on the marshes was' (p. 33). Underdogs can be devoured in more ways than one.

TEXT 2   (PAGE 221)

'When did you come to town, Mr Gargery?'

'Were it yesterday afternoon?' said Joe, after coughing behind his hand, as if he had had time to catch the whooping-cough since he came. 'No it were not. Yes it were. Yes. It were yesterday afternoon' (with an appearance of mingled wisdom, relief, and strict impartiality).

'Have you seen anything of London, yet?'

'Why, yes, Sir,' said Joe, 'me and Wopsle went off straight to look at the Blacking Ware'us. But we didn't find that it come up to its likeness in the red bills at the shop doors; which I meantersay,' added Joe, in an explanatory manner, 'as it is there drawd too architectooralooral.'

> **CONTEXT**
>
> 'Little Britain', a street near the Law Courts and the old Smithfield meat-market, still exists but the **symbolic** significance of the name is obvious.

I really believe Joe would have prolonged this word (mightily expressive to my mind of some architecture that I know) into a perfect Chorus, but for his attention being providentially attracted by his hat, which was toppling. Indeed, it demanded from him a constant attention, and a quickness of eye and hand, very like that exacted by wicket-keeping. He made extraordinary play with it, and showed the greatest skill; now, rushing at it and catching it neatly as it dropped; now, merely stopping it midway, beating it up, and humouring it in various parts of the room and against a good deal of the pattern of the paper on the wall, before he felt it safe to close with it; finally, splashing it into the slop-basin, where I took the liberty of laying hands upon it.

As to his shirt-collar, and his coat-collar, they were perplexing to reflect upon – insoluble mysteries both. Why should a man scrape himself to that extent, before he could consider himself full dressed? Why should he suppose it necessary to be purified by suffering for his holiday clothes? Then he fell into such unaccountable fits of meditation, with his fork midway between his plate and his mouth; had his eyes attracted in such strange directions; was afflicted with such remarkable coughs; sat so far from the table, and dropped so much more than he ate, and pretended that he hadn't dropped it; that I was heartily glad when Herbert left us for the city.

CHECK THE NET

For discussion of education as an important Dickensian theme see: **http://www. umd.umich.edu/ casl/hum/eng/ classes/434/ geweb/**

I had neither the good sense nor the good feeling to know that this was all my fault, and that if I had been easier with Joe, Joe would have been easier with me. I felt impatient of him and out of temper with him; in which condition he heaped coals of fire on my head.

'Us two being now alone, Sir,' – began Joe.

'Joe,' I interrupted, pettishly, 'how can you call me Sir?'

Joe looked at me for a single instant with something faintly like reproach. Utterly preposterous as his cravat was, and as his collars were, I was conscious of a sort of dignity in the look.

'Us two being now alone,' resumed Joe, 'and me having the intention and abilities to stay not many minutes more, I will now conclude – leastways begin – to mention what have led to my having had the present honour. For was it not,' said Joe, with his old air of lucid exposition, 'that my only wish were to be useful to you, I should not have had the honour of breaking wittles in the company and abode of gentlemen.'

I was so unwilling to see the look again, that I made no remonstrance against this tone.

This passage is taken from Chapter 27 when Joe visits Pip in London to tell him of Estella's return to Satis House. Pip is now a gentleman living in lodgings with Herbert who is the first speaker. This is another meal scene which we might compare with others in the past and to come. In Chapter 2, Pip tells how he and Joe compared the bites in their bread wedges in 'good-natured companionship' (p. 11), and during the Christmas dinner Joe sought to comfort Pip, however ineffectually. We can measure Pip's decline into snobbery by his critical attitude to Joe here. Herbert attempts to put Joe at his ease, and we remember how he educated Pip in genteel table manners when he first arrived in London (Chapter 22). Pip may now be a gentleman, but he does not act like a gentle man. His distaste for Joe's clumsy eating here will be nothing in comparison to his disgust at Magwitch's 'heavy grubbing' (p. 331) in Chapter 40. But his fastidiousness will be of no purpose then. His pretensions to gentility will be exposed.

Clothes imagery is important. Going to church on the marshes, Joe and Pip were both dressed up in their unsuitable, uncomfortable Sunday 'penitentials' (Chapter 4, p. 23), but Pip chooses to forget that now, and feigns astonishment at Joe's awkward attire. He forgets too how Herbert looked more stylish in his old clothes, than he, newly arrived, did in Trabb's 'local work' (p. 152). Clothes become symbolic of identity. Later in the chapter Joe will admit he is 'wrong in these clothes' (p. 224). He has tried to assume a false role in deference to Pip's rise in social status, but it hasn't been a success. Dress acts as a barrier and emphasises the superficial differences made by money and class. Pip judges Joe by inappropriate criteria as a 'failed' gentleman because he feels insecure in his own position.

CHECK THE FILM

Note that in David Lean's 1946 film Pip goes out to meet Joe rather than wait and let him struggle to find the right chambers, thus making his character rather more sympathetic.

Pip's position as narrator is divided. It is partly that of the young Mr Pip at the time, and partly that of the older, wiser Philip Pirrip looking back, judging himself as he once criticised Joe. The latter is particularly evident in the paragraph where he admits that 'this was all my fault'. The reference to Joe 'heaping coals of fire on my head' is biblical, taken from Romans 12:20, and refers to the pain that the innocent can inflict on their enemies by returning good for evil.

Pip's language is elegant and superior, both in phrasing and vocabulary. Examples include: 'mightily expressive of some architecture that I know'; 'providentially attracted'; 'took the liberty of laying hands'; 'perplexing to reflect upon'; 'insoluble mysteries both'; 'utterly preposterous'; 'old air of lucid exposition'; 'no remonstrance'; 'in an explanatory manner'. It is the language of a gentleman, polysyllabic, Latinate, carefully grammatical, and it asserts the power of social and cultural advantage.

In contrast, Joe's speech represents a parody of this kind of style. The choice of pronouns is often wrong ('us' instead of 'we'), and auxiliary verbs do not agree with their subjects ('were it yesterday'; 'what have led to'). Tenses and syntax get confused, 'h's dropped, and words mispronounced ('Blacking Ware'us'; 'as it is there drawd too architectooralooral'). In his efforts to be polite, Joe fails to find the appropriate level of formality and sounds comically stiff ('I should not have had the honour of breaking wittles in the company and abode of gentlemen'). Joe's speech is akin to his dress: it is uncomfortable and it does not fit him. It will be a different matter when he casts false ceremony aside at the end of the chapter.

Joe's problems with his hat are comic but symbolic too. He juggles with his hat much as he does with his syntax; they both represent his social insecurity. Dickens gets his comic effect by slowing down the action and drawing it out in long, elaborate sentences. The humour comes partly from **irony**; Pip calls Joe a skilled wicket-keeper when he is obviously not, only very clumsy. It also comes from making the hat have a life of its own. Joe 'beats' it and 'humours' it before he feels safe 'to close with it'. This is a comic use of **personification**.

CHECK THE BOOK

For a moving account of Dickens' experiences in the blacking warehouse, see John Forster's *Life of Charles Dickens* (1872–74), Chapter 2.

Joe, with his coughing and vacant stares, is made to look a fool in this passage; he is amusing but it is Pip that we judge. Joe's visit to 'the Blacking Ware'us' is a comic priority for any visitor to London, but there is a hidden biographical reference too. Dickens worked for four months in a blacking factory as a child (see **Background: Charles Dickens**), a humiliation he never forgot and kept a close secret. Its reappearance here suggests he is exploring his own painful memories of social insecurity as he describes Pip's attempt to suppress his.

When Joe next comes to London, it will be to pay Pip's debts and nurse him back to health (Chapter 57). For a while, the old childhood intimacy will revive, but Joe will still eventually call Pip 'Sir'. This time, Pip will genuinely regret, but better understand, the irretrievable consequences of broken links and ties.

TEXT 3   (PAGES 401–2)

Taking the brewery on my way back, I raised the rusty latch of a little door at the garden end of it, and walked through. I was going out at the opposite door – not easy to open now, for the damp wood had started and swelled, and the hinges were yielding, and the threshold was encumbered with a growth of fungus – when I turned my head to look back. A childish association revived with wonderful force in the moment of the slight action, and I fancied that I saw Miss Havisham hanging to the beam. So strong was the impression, that I stood under the beam shuddering from head to foot before I knew it was a fancy – though to be sure I was there in an instant.

The mournfulness of the place and time, and the great terror of this illusion, though it was but momentary, caused me to feel an indescribable awe as I came out between the open wooden gates where I had once wrung my hair after Estella had wrung my heart. Passing on into the front court-yard, I hesitated whether to call the woman to let me out at the locked gate of which she had the key, or first to go up-stairs and assure myself that Miss Havisham was as safe and well as I had left her. I took the latter course and went up.

I looked into the room where I had left her, and I saw her seated in the ragged chair upon the hearth close to the fire, with her back towards me. In the moment when I was withdrawing my head to go quietly away, I saw a great flaming light spring up. In the same moment, I saw her running at me, shrieking, with a whirl of fire blazing all about her, and soaring at least as many feet above her head as she was high.

I had a double-caped great-coat on, and over my arm another thick coat. That I got them off, closed with her, threw her down, and got them over her; that I dragged the great cloth from the table for the same purpose, and with it dragged down the heap of rottenness in the midst, and all the ugly things that sheltered there; that we were on the ground struggling like desperate enemies, and that the closer I covered her, the more wildly she shrieked and tried to free herself; that this occurred I knew through the result, but not through anything I felt, or thought, or knew I did. I knew nothing until I knew that we were on the floor by the great table, and that patches of tinder yet alight were floating in the smoky air, which, a moment ago, had been her faded bridal dress.

Then I looked round and saw the disturbed beetles and spiders running away over the floor, and the servants coming in with breathless cries at the door. I still held her forcibly down with all my strength, like a prisoner who might escape; and I doubt if I even knew who she was, or why we had struggled, or that she had been in flames, or that the flames were out, until I saw the

CHECK THE NET
Constructed by students at the University of Michigan–Dearborn, *Pip's World: A Hypertext on Charles Dickens' Great Expectations* at **http://www. umich.edu/casl/ hum/eng/classes/ 434/geweb/** has a number of background projects on the text.

patches of tinder that had been her garments, no longer alight but falling in a black shower around us.

Taken from Chapter 49, this passage is part of Pip's final visit to Satis House. He now knows the true source of his expectations and is planning to get Magwitch out of the country. Estella is married to Drummle. Miss Havisham has asked him to come on a matter of business and agreed to give Pip the nine hundred pounds necessary to secure Herbert's partnership with Clarriker. She is much changed and begs Pip's forgiveness. After his interview, Pip revisits the ruined garden with a presentiment that he will not come again.

Pip's life has been determined by his childhood experiences at Satis House quite as much as those in the graveyard on the marsh. He has never lost his 'poor dream' of marrying Estella, or freed himself from Miss Havisham's influence. Throughout his stay in London, he found himself regularly drawn back to the house (Chapters 29, 38 and 44). Memories of his childhood pain still haunt him in this passage as he passes through the brewery where he had once 'wrung' his hair as Estella had 'wrung' his heart, a sad, rueful shift from the literal to the **metaphorical**. The rotten wood, rusty latch and growing fungus are as much expressive of his own decayed hopes and melancholy now as they are of Miss Havisham's. She had seen in him earlier a mirror-image of herself when her heart was broken by Compeyson.

Haunted by the past, Pip experiences the old childish terror of seeing Miss Havisham hanging on a beam, as he did in his first visit (Chapter 8). This gives him a premonition that sends him back to see if she is safe. She is where he had left her, but the moment he withdraws she springs up covered in fire.

Pip's narration in the passage is entirely internal. There is no dialogue. We experience these events like those in a dream; they have a surreal intensity. The apparition of Miss Havisham hanging from a beam returned to haunt Pip from the past and the burning Miss Havisham that runs 'shrieking' towards him with flames high above her head in the present moment seem much the same. Are they both real, or are they both figments of his imagination? The

CHECK THE NET

The Dickens Page is a wide-ranging site with up-to-date information:
http://www.lang. nagoya-u.ac.jp/~ matsuoka/Dickens .html

division between past and present, dream fantasy and daytime reality are blurred. The fact that Miss Havisham bursts into flames the moment he withdraws suggests that somehow he is responsible. Earlier he told her that he forgave her, but can we be sure? Is this his revenge, a wish-fulfilment nightmare apart from his conscious, moral self?

This passage shows Dickens' ability to propel the reader into a world that is magical, **melodramatic** and larger than ordinary daily experience. Like the other Satis House chapters, it moves into fantasy and dream. It suggests that Pip must destroy Miss Havisham and all that she stands for before he can move on himself. It is part of the elaborate process of acceptance and rejection which constitutes the third stage of the novel. In 'saving' Miss Havisham (actually we will never see her again), Pip is, at one level, acting out the role of the young knight of romance that he once thought he was (Chapter 29). Instead of marrying the princess, however, he is killing the wicked witch.

The imagery in this passage is sufficiently ambiguous to support this kind of rather extreme interpretation. It is full of conflict. At one level Pip describes an act of selfless heroism but, at another, the language he uses suggests an assault. He 'closes' with her and 'throws her down'. The two struggle 'like desperate enemies'; Miss Havisham shrieks 'wildly' and tries 'to free herself'. Pip holds her 'forcibly down with all my strength, like a prisoner who might escape' which is reminiscent of the two convicts on the marsh in Chapter 5 and anticipates their final struggle in the water in Chapter 54.

The nightmare quality of the experience is emphasised by Pip's trance-like confusion: 'I knew nothing until I knew we were on the floor'; 'I doubt if I even knew who she was, or why we had struggled'. Time is slowed in suspension like the remnants of Miss Havisham's bridal dress that float burning in the air above them before falling as a black shower on to the floor. This effect is achieved by the way phrases are repeated and echoed at the end of the last two paragraphs: 'patches of timber yet alight were floating …'; 'patches of timber …, no longer alight but falling …'.

CONTEXT

The last phrase of Chapter 19 ('the world lay spread before me' p. 160) echoes Milton's lines 'The world was all before them, where to chose / Their place of rest and providence their guide' at the end of *Paradise Lost*. The original refers to Adam and Eve leaving paradise after the Fall, so its echo is significant: it suggests a loss of innocence and Pip's banishment from a kind of Eden.

CHECK THE NET
For a general Dickens site try David Perdue's *Charles Dickens Page* at **http://www.fidnet.com/%7Edap1955/dickens/**.

The great cloth that Pip pulls from the table, the 'heap of rottenness', the faded bridal dress, 'and all the ugly things', are symbols of Miss Havisham's corrupted existence; they will destroy her and they must be destroyed along with her before new life can begin. The beetles and spiders run away as the servants rush in from the door. Suddenly there is movement where once there had been only stasis.

For Pip this seems a necessary ordeal. He is purifying part of himself. Fire can be domestic and comforting, like Joe's furnace at the forge. Here it is purgatorial, painful (he burns his hand) and cleansing.

PART THREE

CRITICAL APPROACHES

CHARACTERISATION

Dickens is famous for his gift for creating characters who become household names and seem to have a life independent of the books in which they appear. In this novel Miss Havisham has become a type for the embittered woman, disappointed in love and withdrawn from the world; Pumblechook is another type for the pompous, hypocritical braggart. The novelist, E. M. Forster, made a famous distinction between 'flat' characters who are immediately recognisable by their visual presentation and habits of speech, and 'round' characters who are capable of development, and can surprise us. Seen in this way, many of Dickens' characters seem to be 'flat'. We can learn more about them, but when they show change, like Miss Havisham's repentance or Jaggers' sympathy for the infant Estella, we may not be easily convinced. It is not where the energy of the presentation resides.

Dickens was a serial novelist and needed to make his characters instantly recognisable and memorable for readers taking up his stories after the break of a week or a month. To do this, he learnt much from the popular theatre of the day. There are many characters in *Great Expectations* who announce themselves by their distinctive use of language or external appearance. Good examples of the former would be Joe's 'what larks', 'ever the best of friends' and bumbling 'meantersay's, Drummle's sneering 'Oh Lord!'s and Jaggers' fierce 'Now's and 'Very well's. Such verbal mannerisms are just part of the way in which Dickens displays his characters through their own distinctive vocabulary and syntax. Visual display is also important and serves the same purpose. Jaggers' habit of biting his thumb or compulsive hand-washing, Wemmick's 'post-office' (Chapter 21, p. 172) mouth or the distracted Matthew Pocket attempting to lift himself up by his own hair are the signs by which we know these characters but also suggest an inner life to which we have no access.

CHECK THE BOOK

Forster's distinction between `flat' and 'round' chararacters can be found in the chapter entitled `People' in *Aspect of the Novel* (1927).

Dickens' external treatment of character in this way was a great gift. It is sometimes called **caricature** but that is not to imply that it is crude or unsubtle. It is often used to make a point about a particular weakness or obsession, or to suggest how people learn to function in an aggressive, competitive society.

QUESTION

The name 'Pip' means 'a seed': discuss the hero's growth from childhood to maturity in *Great Expectations*.

Not all of Dickens' characters are constructed in this way. For example, Herbert and Biddy are less emphatic or eccentric in their presentation. Biddy is a skilful study in understatement, shrewd and morally tough in everything she says, while Herbert convinces as a good man who only needs his chance to make his way in life. However, it is true to say that Dickens is imaginatively excited by the extremes in the human condition. Orlick is a black villain with no redeeming feature, and Joe is the innocent man-child, part saint and part unconscious comedian.

Because of his strength in depicting human excess and eccentricity from an external point of view, Dickens is sometimes criticised for an inability to make characters develop or change convincingly. To use Forster's definition, he is weak in creating 'round' characters with a convincing inner life. An example often cited is Estella's discovery of a heart in the final chapter which seems driven more by the demands of plot than inner necessity, but Magwitch's 'softening' and stoical dignity in the final phase of this novel is very persuasive.

Of course, the most complex character in the book is Pip himself. In a sense, he *is* the book: everything we know is filtered through his consciousness. He is the narrator of his own 'great expectations' and shows Dickens' talent as a psychologist to the full. Writing his own life in an attempt to master and understand it, Pip demonstrates a wide range of human emotions from repressed rage through baffled desire to saddened acceptance. His frustrated attempt to deny his own past, his guilt, insecurity and bad faith, are all confessed unsparingly. Pip gains his authority as a narrator by being close to Dickens himself. Indeed, he seems to become one with his creator in some of the more exuberant, comic set-pieces like Mrs Joe's funeral, Trabb's boy's performance or Wopsle's *Hamlet*. By making Pip come to terms with himself by learning to accept Magwitch, it seems likely that Dickens is using Pip as a **persona** through which he can explore his own sense of guilt for past misdeeds and express his hopes of becoming a better man.

It is sometimes helpful to view Dickens' characterisation strategically across a book, rather than simply view characters as individuals. He will often use characterisation to develop a theme, or as variations on an idea. For example, Wopsle and Orlick shadow Pip throughout his career as a gentleman and act as cruder examples of the notion of 'bettering oneself'. Orlick, Drummle, Trabb's boy and 'Pepper', Pip's servant in London, all seem to exaggerate and parody certain undesirable elements in his character. Orlick and Drummle, in particular, are dark doubles at opposite ends of the social scale who seem to act out Pip's potential for evil. They punish those who have caused Pip pain. Drummle mistreats Estella. Orlick humiliates Pumblechook and returns Mrs Joe's violence with a weapon that Pip has, however inadvertently, provided.

CHECK THE BOOK

For a discussion of what Julian Moynahan calls the complex unity of 'Pip-Orlick' see his essay, 'The Hero's Guilt: The Case of *Great Expectations*' (1960), anthologised in Norman Page's Macmilllan Casebook on the novel.

THEMES

SPEAKING AND WRITING

Great Expectations is an 'education novel' or **bildungsroman** and Pip's story begins with his attempt to read himself into an identity from family inscriptions on a tombstone. The narrative is primarily concerned with Pip's efforts to 'read' and understand his situation, his evolving place in a strange and hostile world. The novel is a retrospective, confessional narrative by a now literate man who once called himself Pip, 'and came to be called Pip' (Chapter 1, p. 3). Speaking and writing are the means by which we create and sustain our identities. In the modern world literacy is an essential skill for self-development and in Victorian England it was the path to social progress and individual advancement. Mrs Joe knows this well and keeps Joe illiterate for she 'is given to government,' Joe explains, and is 'not over partial to my being a scholar, for fear I might rise' (Chapter 7, p. 49). Pip suffers social shame through 'calling the knaves, Jacks' (Chapter 8, p. 60) quite as much as by his coarse hands and thick boots.

**CHECK
THE BOOK**
For more
background on
education see Philip
Collins' *Dickens and
Education* (1963).

Mastery of language is the key to the social mobility so essential to Pip in his ambition to become a gentleman, and literacy is the skill that separates him from his two foster fathers, Joe and Magwitch. Both show parental pride in Pip's attainments in language. In Chapter 7 there is comedy in Joe's admiration for Pip's rudimentary ability with the chalk and slate; by Chapter 40, Magwitch is happy to hear Pip read foreign languages he cannot understand. This regard of the unlettered for culture contrasts with the well-born but loutish gentleman, Bentley Drummle, 'who took up a book as if its writer had done him an injury' (Chapter 25, p. 202).

However, there are losses as well as gains in the standardization of language that literacy entails. Rich oral traditions and local dialects fade away before the power of the centralising nation state. Dickens, looking back to his childhood from the vantage point of the 1860s is celebrating a past that is gone for ever. Pip first feels a superiority to Joe when he discovers that he cannot read and there is much comedy to be had when Joe struggles to express himself in complex, unfamiliar social situations. But Joe's moral instinct is never wrong and he can express himself well enough when it matters: '"And bring the poor little child. God bless the poor little child," I said to your sister, "there's room for *him* at the forge!"' (Chapter 7, p. 48). The paradox is, of course, that it needs a literate Pip to remember such sayings and to write them down.

Joe and Biddy are the conservative centre of this novel, content to fill their place at the forge with honour and dignity. Joe has capacity enough to learn what he needs to learn and, unlike Mrs Joe, Biddy is a good teacher. On his first visit to London, Joe can barely decipher the name on Pip's door; by the time he comes again to rescue Pip from his debtors he can write, comically and laboriously maybe, a parting note of simple dignity that finally matches the best of his speech.

GENTLEMEN AND GENTLE MEN

When Pip goes to Satis House he learns he is 'a common labouring-boy' (Chapter 8, p. 60). Henceforth the dominant purpose in his life will be to become a gentleman and win Estella. Money seems to buy him the status of a gentleman. When he is about to leave the forge, his new clothes bring new respect from Trabb and Pumblechook but not from those who love him (Chapter 19). In time he learns the superficial habits of a gentleman, but he doesn't behave in a gentlemanly way when Joe visits him in London (Chapter 27) or when Trabb's boy mocks him on his return to the town (Chapter 30). Herbert Pocket and his father have the tactful instincts of gentlemen, even when they are quite poor, while Drummle is a stupid, cruel man, though he is clearly a gentleman in social terms. Dickens shows us that the life of a 'brought-up London gentleman' (Chapter 39, p. 321), can be idle and dissipated, corrupting Pip's better instincts. Dickens further develops this theme through Magwitch's hatred of Compeyson (Chapter 42), who is a gentleman in style but the source of so much evil in the book. In contrast, Joe is an instinctively gentle man although he can deal with the evil Orlick (Chapter 15) or the bullying Jaggers (Chapter 18) if he has to. His humane response to Magwitch on the marshes (Chapter 5) contrasts markedly with cruelty and oppression around him. He may look absurd in his Sunday clothes but Pip's recognition of him as 'a gentle Christian man' (Chapter 57, p. 463) marks Pip's moral regeneration and escape from false gentility.

There is some discussion of blacksmiths and the significance of this work in the novel at **http://www.umd.umich.edu/casl/hum/eng/classes/434/geweb/** under 'Work and Social Class'.

INDUSTRY AND IDLENESS

Dickens belonged to a new generation of Victorian self-made men and had an instinctive mistrust of inherited wealth. One definition of a gentleman in the social sense meant having no profession and living a life of idleness. As Magwitch says proudly, 'I lived rough, that you should live smooth; I worked hard, that you should be above work' (Chapter 39, p. 319). Without meaningful work, Pip soon falls into debt and dissipation. His realisation that he is in danger of corrupting Herbert, and his efforts to buy him a partnership in business, marks the beginning of his moral regeneration. Dickens was anxious to point out the moral by making Pip's final place in life that of a bourgeois business man. As he wrote in his working notes: 'the one good thing he did in his prosperity, the only thing that endures and bears good fruit.' Like many of his contemporaries, Dickens wished to shift the definition of a gentleman away from notions of class and polished manners to one that emphasised social responsibility and vocational commitment.

Dickens was also interested in the nature of work and its effects on people's lives. The main focus for this in *Great Expectations* is the criminal law. Jaggers is the complete professional, ruthless and competent, who, save a brief confession in Chapter 50, never lets down his guard. His life is devoted to secrets, power and manipulation. He has no private life. Wemmick is rather different. He manages to function by dividing himself into two people, the office Wemmick devoted to 'portable property' and the loving, kindly Wemmick of the Walworth castle. Of course Joe Gargery at the forge is the image of unalienated labour, happy and contented in his work. It is an image of nostalgic appeal that looks increasingly remote from the harsher realities of the new urban life of the nineteenth century. Some critics have felt that Dickens evades some of his own criticisms of the modern city as a place of ruthless exploitation by allowing Pip to make his money in the discreet safety of a business house abroad.

 CHECK THE NET

There is further discussion of crime, prisons and public executions under 'Prisons, Crime and the Law' at **http:// www.umd.umich. edu/casl/hum/eng/ classes/434/geweb/**

RESPECTABILITY AND CRIME

In the novel's opening chapters, the wild, exposed marshes are put into arresting juxtaposition with the smug, self-satisfied Christmas dinner at the forge. Because of his theft, Pip feels more kinship with the starving convict outside than those within; when the soldiers arrive, he thinks their manacles are for him (Chapter 4). Thus, from the beginning, Pip's conscious struggles for gentility are shadowed by a sense of his own criminality. When he is 'bound' by his indentures as an apprentice, someone gives him a pamphlet 'TO BE READ IN MY CELL' (Chapter 13, p. 105) and he feels obscurely responsible for his sister's assault (Chapter 16).

When he goes to London, Pip's past continues to haunt him. His life as a gentleman is financed through Jaggers' office where the death masks of criminals look down from the walls. On his visit to Satis House in Chapter 28, he discovers convicts on the coach, recognises one as the stranger in the Three Jolly Bargemen with the file (Chapter 10), and overhears their conversation on the two pound notes. His benefactor had stipulated that he must always keep the name of Pip, but he is grateful that Herbert had addressed him as 'Handel'. When he meets Estella off the London coach (Chapter 32), Pip wishes he could escape the past as he brushes the dust of Newgate off his clothes.

So when Magwitch finally reappears (Chapter 39), it seems as if his shocking revelation has been obscurely known all along. Pip's expectations are only different from Wemmick's 'portable property' in their scale; both are obtained from criminals. These links between fashionable social life and the criminal underworld are underlined by the plot. Satis House and the marshes are not as far apart as we first suppose. Compeyson moves in both social and criminal circles; Jaggers is lawyer to Miss Havisham and Magwitch. Pip discovers not only that his fortunes are founded on the labour of a criminal, but also that his guiding 'star', Estella, is the daughter of a felon and a murderess. In linking the two worlds of the novel in this way, Dickens is suggesting that the riches and privileges of the few are gained by the exclusion and exploitation of the many.

PARENTS AND CHILDREN

The novel opens with the young Pip weeping by his parents' grave and much of the drama of his life story evolves around his relationship with parental figures. Back at the forge, Mrs Joe brings him up 'by hand' (Chapter 2, p. 7) while a loving, but ineffectual stepfather is helpless to intervene. Other adults seek the role of step-parent in order to use and exploit Pip for their own purposes. Magwitch leaps up from behind his parents' tombstone to force him into crime while Miss Havisham sees in him an easy prey for Estella to practise her cruel, capricious nature, and a tool to torment the greedy Pocket relatives.

The power of family ties and obligations is a significant force for good and evil in *Great Expectations*. Magwitch adopts Pip for mixed motives. Partly he wishes to express his gratitude, but he also wants to 'own' a 'brought-up London gentleman' (Chapter 39, p. 321) as an expression of contempt for the establishment that has ostracised him. Miss Havisham takes in the baby Estella for benevolent reasons but cannot help but turn her into a weapon for her revenge on men (Chapter 49). Thus Pip and Estella are corrupted siblings as much as potential lovers; both are the victims of the plots and schemes of parental figures that chance has brought their way.

Dickens further develops the theme of familial love and neglect for comic purposes. The delightful Walworth scenes (Chapters 25 and 37)

? QUESTION

Discuss Pip's loss and discovery of father figures as an important theme in *Great Expectations*.

CHECK THE BOOK
Journal articles on the treatment of violence, especially violence on women and children, in *Great Expectations* are conveniently anthologised in Roger D. Sell's edited collection in the Macmillan New Casebook series.

where Wemmick humours 'the Aged' contrast with Bill Barley's tyrannical treatment of his daughter Clara (Chapter 46), and Pip's early corrections by 'Tickler' (Chapter 2) may be compared with the more benign neglect of the chaotic Pocket household (Chapters 23 and 33). Pip can only be healed of his early pain by the acceptance of his criminal stepfather, Magwitch, and by forgiving Miss Havisham (Chapter 49). This will lead to his final reconciliation with Joe, the one parental figure who loves him unconditionally. The novel ends with hope for a better future in the figure of 'little Pip', Joe and Biddy's child. He will have the benefit of wholesome parental love and, in Pip, a kind and understanding godfather.

BEATING AND CRINGING

Discussing Bentley Drummle and the likely outcome of his marriage to Estella, Jaggers declares that 'A fellow like our friend the Spider ... either beats, or cringes' (Chapter 48, p. 390), a view immediately and obediently endorsed by Wemmick. Most of the characters in the book could be divided into 'beaters' or 'cringers'. Sometimes beaters become cringers, or cringers learn to become beaters. Wemmick is subservient to Jaggers in his chambers, but becomes a beater himself when undertaking Jaggers' business outside. Bullying Uncle Pumblechook soon becomes a cringer when Pip has his 'expectations'. Issues of power, economic, social and psychological, are at the heart of *Great Expectations*.

Young Pip's beatings, physical and emotional, are intense and unremitting in the early chapters. Threatened by cannibalistic Magwitch, 'Ram-paged' by 'Tickler' (Chapter 2), told he is 'Naterally wicious' (Chapter 4, p. 26) by Mr Hubble at the Christmas dinner table and taunted by Estella, small wonder he is 'morally timid and very sensitive' (Chapter 8, p. 63). However much we would like to see Joe as the ideal father that Pip rejected, we cannot ignore his failure to protect Pip because of his own early treatment as a child. This is a failure he recognises, and so he seeks, somewhat inarticulately, to make amends for this during their final reconciliation in Chapter 57.

Pip internalises his sufferings into a passive victimhood that expresses itself most strongly in his hopeless love for Estella. He faithfully follows Miss Havisham's masochistic exhortations to give up 'your whole life and soul to the smiter – as I did' (Chapter 29, p. 240). Miss Havisham is a cringer who learns to become a beater and then, abjectly under Estella's cold rejection, a pathetic cringer again: 'She turned her face to me for the first time since she had averted it, and, to my amazement, I may even add to my terror, dropped on her knees at my feet' (Chapter 49, p. 398).

Representatives of crime and the law, the two most ferocious beaters in the novel are Orlick and Jaggers, and both carry out their most extreme punishments on women. Orlick terrorises and tortures Pip, but he murders Mrs Joe. Jaggers intimidates in court, but he has 'a wild beast tamed' (Chapter 24, p. 202) at home in the person of his housekeeper Molly – and he tames her in a manner that is impressively sinister because it is unspecified.

In fact there is a pattern of strong women dominated, tamed and broken in the novel. Biddy and Clara are the Victorian ideal of domesticated, caring and accepting womanhood, but most of Dickens' imaginative energy, it seems, goes into angry, assertive and embittered women that he then, by proxy, seeks to dominate and control. Mrs Joe wants mastery at the forge but Orlick punishes her with a terrible blow that brings her to submission. In a grim **parody** of the chalk and slate scene between Joe and Pip in Chapter 7, Mrs Joe traces the sign of Orlick's hammer to summons him into her presence: 'She watched his countenance as if she were particularly wishful to be assured that he took kindly to his reception, she showed every possible desire to conciliate him, and there was an air of humble propitiation in all she did, such as I have seen pervade the bearing of a child towards a hard master' (Chapter 16, p. 124).

Estella's beauty may draw 'Moths and all sorts of ugly creatures' into the candle flame of her beauty (Chapter 38, p. 310), but she too must be 'bent and broken' into 'a better shape' (Chapter 59, p. 484) by Bentley Drummle, or so she submissively hopes, before she and Pip can be allowed to walk away into the future.

www. CHECK THE NET
Further discussion of the matter of violent women and violence between the sexes can be found under 'Women' at: **http:// umd.umich.edu/ casl/hum/eng/ classes/434/geweb/**

NARRATIVE TECHNIQUES

STRUCTURE

Great Expectations is structured in three stages. These correspond to the three volumes of the first edition but they are integral to the overall organisation of the text and not just to publishing expediency. One pattern that may be discerned is the Christian one of innocence, fall and sin, and final redemption through expiation and suffering. Dickens was an instinctive Christian and thought in religious terms. Pip must lose the world (at least temporarily) in order to regain his soul. In several key episodes like the discovery of his expectations (Chapter 19), the burial of Mrs Joe (Chapter 35) and the death of Magwitch (Chapter 56), biblical references are used to make an ironical or moral point. The use of the Miltonic phrase 'the world lay spread before me' (Chapter 19, p. 160) which ends the first stage of the novel is clearly designed to suggest Pip's departure from the forge is analogous to the expulsion of Adam and Eve from Eden.

> **CONTEXT**
>
> The reference to 'the Eastern story' (Chapter 38) is to one of James Ridley's *Tales of the Genii* (1776), a great favourite of the young Dickens. The story implies the collapse of Pip's hopes and the destruction of an impostor.

Another, quite different, narrative strategy in highlighted by the reference to the crushing slab in the 'Eastern Story' near the end of the second stage of the novel (Chapter 38). Some of the greatest and most significant stories in Western literature, like *Oedipus Rex* and *Macbeth*, contain a moment of recognition and reversal of fortune. The hero has pursued a course of action, on the basis of knowledge and understanding, which events suddenly reveal is false. The hero's plans are shown to be useless, his hopes and aspirations futile or self-destructive. He has been deceived all along. Clearly much of the power of Pip's narrative is gained by Dickens structuring his story along these lines.

Finally, Dickens' story can be read as a kind of moral **fable** illustrating the dangers and possibilities inherent in a newly affluent, competitive society. Pip is torn away from his roots at the forge, comes to no good in London but receives an education and other social advantages. When disaster strikes, he discovers that there is no going back to his simple origins but, sadder and wiser, he is able to prosper as a businessman overseas by using his own talents instead of living corruptly off inherited, unearned money.

PLOTS

At the beginning of the novel, Pip is the victim of the plotting of others. Not only do Magwitch and Miss Havisham have plans for him, but some of the minor characters cast him in dubious roles for their own entertainment, too. Wopsle sees him as the Prodigal Son in the Bible story (Chapter 4) or Barnwell the apprentice murderer (Chapter 15); Pumblechook insists on casting him as his ungrateful protégé.

CHECK THE BOOK
G. Robert Stang's essay 'Expectations Well Lost: Dickens's Fable for His Time', *College English,* 16 (October 1954), pp. 9–17 takes this view. Extracts from this essay can be found in Tredell's *Reader's Guide.*

Until Magwitch's reappearance in Chapter 39, Pip consistently misreads the nature of the plot he is in. He thinks that he is the changeling of fairy tale who is really of noble birth. Miss Havisham is a fairy godmother, and Estella an enchanted princess imprisoned in Satis House. It is his destiny to rescue her. The reality proves to be different. Miss Havisham is the wicked witch after all, and Estella a genuine ice-maiden. Pip needs to be cured of his day-dreaming romanticism. His wealth has no magical source; London streets are not paved with gold, but squalid, criminal and treacherous. Magwitch's plot is repressed but keeps surfacing fitfully in ominous signs and omens like the reappearance of the file, the two 'sweltering' pound notes (Chapter 10, p. 78), or the convicts on the coach.

Part of the appeal of *Great Expectations* is that it contains a false romantic plot and an ironically realist one and they interact with each other. Once Pip is fully aware of his true situation, he becomes an active plotter in his own right. He schemes to hide and save Magwitch and, playing the detective, he unearths the secret of Estella's parentage, which even Jaggers does not know. The story is made from a web of plots, some embedded in others: the fate of Pip and Estella is already determined by plots hatched by Arthur, Miss Havisham's half-brother, and the arch villain Compeyson, many years before the story opens. One particularly sensational plot, adding to the excitement in the final stages of the novel, is Orlick's revenge in the sluicehouse, also aided by Compeyson.

HALLUCINATIONS, NIGHTMARES AND INTIMATIONS

From the start of his search into the 'identity of things' (Chapter 1, p. 3), the reader follows Pip's progress as he moves through a world of confusing and conflicting signs. Part of the evolving drama in the novel is the way that Pip wilfully 'misreads' clues to the origin of his expectations. Guilt and a sense of culpability are indelibly printed on his consciousness from the beginning and for most of the narrative he seeks to repress them. He is in denial about his early 'criminal' past and finds it imposible to confess to Joe. When Magwitch finally reveals himself as the source of Pip's expectations in the magnificent Chapter 39, Pip's shock is all the more powerful because we sense that the knowledge has been repressed but obscurely known all along. It has been a necessary and integral part of Pip's guilt-torn personality.

Dickens wrote in an age before psychoanalysis, but his work shows an awareness of dimensions of reality that could be accessed through dreams or moments of heightened perception. These moments are expressed in a language of **gothic** terror or grotesque absurdity. A good example of this is the vision of Miss Havisham hanging from a beam in the disused brewery. Pip's childish sense of a tortured, self-destructive soul is made manifest: 'And my terror was greatest of all, when I found no figure there' (Chapter 8, p. 64). This vision is repeated in Chapter 49 on Pip's final visit to Satis House. This time it is a genuine premonition; Pip returns to the house to find Miss Havisham 'running at me, shrieking, with a whirl of fire blazing all around her, and soaring at least as many feet above her head as she was high' (p. 402). Different planes of perception suddenly fuse together. The reader is disorientated, uncertain what is real, what is nightmare. (See **Extended commentaries: Text 3** for further discussion of this passage.) Something similar occurs with the fearful appearance of Orlick at the sluicehouse four chapters later. Orlick has been stalking Pip from the margins of the text for most of the novel: now suddenly he is centre-stage, transformed by the extreme dark and candlelight into an accusing demon from some other world: 'It was you as did for your shrew sister' (Chapter 53, p. 426).

**CHECK
THE BOOK**
See Steven Connor's
Charles Dickens for
an interesting
discussion of Pip's
delirious dream.

Several chapters end in dreams. In Chapter 2 the fitfully dozing Pip pulls the dramatic events of the day into a dream scenario where Hulks, pirate, gibbet, all images of retribution, appear. In Chapter 10 the unwelcome stranger's file haunts Pip. In his sleep 'I saw the file coming at me out of a door, without seeing who held it, and I screamed myself awake' (p. 79). At the end of Chapter 31 Pip returns from Waldengarver's comic Hamlet to dream 'that my expectations were all cancelled, and that I had to give my hand in marriage to Herbert's Clara, or play Hamlet to Miss Havisham's Ghost, before twenty thousand people, without knowing twenty words of it' (p. 258). This sense of powerlessness, of Pip being caught up in plots over which he has no control or understanding is still more vividly expressed in his hysterical, fever-stricken nightmare in Chapter 57. Pip's delirium here seems to be the psychological equivalent of Orlick's physical torture, a necessary trial he has to endure before he can start to build a new life.

CHECK THE NET

For some possible connections between *Great Expectations* and *Hamlet* see under 'Theatres and Fairs' at: **http://umd. umich.du/casl/ hum/eng/classes/ 434/geweb/**

The process of uncovering and pulling together lost connections also features in the Estella sub-plot. Pip's obscure efforts to discover Estella's identity shadows his unsuccessful courtship of her in the middle section of the novel. 'What *was* it?' (Chapter 29, p. 238), 'What *was* the nameless shadow which once again in that one instant had passed?' (Chapter 32, p. 264). It is significant that Pip's dawning understanding of Estella's parentage should be built around the image of knitting. It is Pip who finally 'knits' the loose ends of the plot together. This is part of the drive for understanding that gives the reader, too, a sense of completeness and wholeness by the end of the novel.

NARRATORS

The story is told by Philip Pirrip, a middle-aged businessman, looking back on the development of his younger self. When novels are written in the omniscient third person, the reader oversees all the action, as the writer does. We do not have this luxury reading *Great Expectations*; we know what Pip knows and are limited by what he chooses to narrate. This novel is a great mystery tale because of this. Pip chooses to believe that Miss Havisham is his benefactor. As readers, we can make different inferences from the evidence he provides, but we do not know the truth until he does. This lends dramatic immediacy to the action.

In Dickens' hands, first person narration is an extremely flexible medium for telling a story. Pip is a brilliant teller of his own tale, comic, dramatic, regretful and ironic by turns. Part of the tension in

QUESTION

At the beginning
of Chapter 33
Estella tells Pip,
'We are not free
to follow our own
devices, you and I'.
(p. 265). How true
is this?

the narration lies in the manner in which the older, wiser Pip reviews the various stages in his past life from frightened child through a romantically troubled adolescence and then to arrogant but anxious adult.

As narrator, Philip Pirrip tries to maintain a detachment from his past self as he attempts to recall past events and his feelings about them, but there is always a tension. The angle of vision shifts; sometimes we are close, sometimes much more distant. We can be in the midst of a dramatic event which the narrator is reliving as little Pip, like the early scenes on the marshes; at other times he is judging his younger self with severity and greater detachment. A good example would be the conversations with Biddy (Chapters 17, 19 and 35) where the narrator simply reports and allows the reader to make the inference.

On other occasions, particularly when he remembers his treatment of Joe, the narrator inserts his own regrets and self-criticisms much more openly. See Chapter 18 when the touch of Joe's hand is compared to 'an angel's wing' (p. 141), or the end of Chapter 29 when he admits how quickly his tears of remorse 'soon dried' (p. 244). But the older 'Mr Pip' can also relate the chaos at Hammersmith or the charming domesticity at Walworth with warmth and humour that convinces us that his better instincts have not been lost in London. Towards the end of the story, he becomes a more active narrator, thinking less of himself and more of others. This, too, points to his moral regeneration.

Pip is not the only narrator. He needs others to provide him with information which he has no means of knowing himself. Events that took place before he was born are recounted by Herbert, who tells of Miss Havisham's past in Chapter 22, and Magwitch in Chapter 42. Magwitch recounts his early life and relations with Compeyson with great gusto. His account of his brutalising childhood and the reasons for his hatred of Compeyson are significant for the development of the social criticism in the novel. Finally, Jaggers, with typical legal caution, fills in the final details necessary for Pip to confirm Estella's parentage (Chapter 51).

ENDINGS

Dickens' first readers liked conclusive, reassuring endings that tied up all the loose ends. It is possible to view all of the third stage of Pip's expectations when he knows who his benefactor is as a prolonged and complicated series of terminal gestures. He gives up all thought of Magwitch's money, forgives Miss Havisham, discovers Estella's parentage and stands by the dying Magwitch; he goes through a purgatorial illness, is reconciled to Joe as a child re-born, and failing to provide himself with a convenient marriage to Biddy, makes his decision to emigrate.

QUESTION

Analyse Orlick's role and purpose in *Great Expectations*.

The final third of the book is full of rewards and punishments, deaths and weddings. Miss Havisham, Magwitch, Compeyson and the inconvenient, crotchety Bill Barley all die; Herbert marries his Clara, Wemmick, the formidable Miss Skiffins, and Joe is rewarded with Biddy. Estella is, more sadly, united with Bentley Drummle. Matthew Pocket gets a handsome legacy, while the other parasite Pockets get derisory sums of money.

It seems appropriate that neither Pip nor Estella should be part of this general settling of accounts: their futures are altogether more problematic. How Dickens decided to resolve their fate is discussed elsewhere (see **Note on the text**) but the final chapter of the novel is interesting for its elegiac, resigned tone. After eleven years, Pip returns to the forge to find 'little Pip' in the fireplace corner where he once sat. Taking him to the gravestone where the whole action began, Pip seems to be placating old ghosts and releasing himself from all demands of plot. 'Little Pip' will have a much less troubled life than he, and, hopefully, no need to write his story.

AMBIGUOUSLY EVER AFTER

The phrase is used by David Lodge in his critical book, *Working with Structuralism* (1981), where he discusses problematic endings to novels. Dickens' original plan was to close the book in an enlarged Chapter 58. A rejected ending follows Biddy's question 'you are sure you don't fret for her?' (p. 481) It runs as follows:

'Dear Pip,' said Biddy, 'you are sure you don't fret for her?'

'I am sure and certain, Biddy.'

'Tell me as an old, old friend. Have you quite forgotten her?'

'My dear Biddy, I have forgotten nothing in my life that ever had a foremost place there. But that poor dream, as I once used to call it, has all gone by, Biddy, all gone by!'

It was two years more, before I saw herself. I had heard of her as leading a most unhappy life, and being separated from her husband who had used her with great cruelty, and who had become quite renown as a compound of pride, brutality, and meanness. I had heard of the death of her husband (from an accident consequent on ill-treating a horse), and of her being married again to a Shropshire doctor, who, against his interest, had once very manfully interposed, on an occasion when he was in professional attendance on Mr Drummle, and witnessed some outrageous treatment of her. I had heard that the Shropshire doctor was not rich, and that they lived on her own personal fortune.

CHECK THE NET

For pictures from a Victorian street atlas that will give some sense of Pip's London see: **http: www.stanford. edu/dept/news/ dickens/**

I was in England again – in London, and walking along Piccadilly with little Pip – when a servant came running after me to ask would I step back to a lady in a carriage who wished to speak to me. It was a little pony carriage, which the lady was driving; and the lady and I looked sadly enough on one another.

'I am greatly changed, I know; but I thought you would like to shake hands with Estella too, Pip. Lift up that pretty child and let me kiss it!' (She supposed the child, I think, to be my child.)

I was very glad afterwards to have had the interview; for, in her face and in her voice, and in her touch, she gave me the assurance, that suffering had been stronger than Miss Havisham's teaching , and had given her a heart to understand what my heart used to be.

This bleak aftermath has been felt by some to be a more fitting end to Pip's story. He has lost his financial 'expectations', and it seems appropriate that he should lose Estella too. This ending reads like an exhausted afterthought. The meeting in the street has a very modern tone; it is a brief, casual meeting and misunderstandings prevail. Estella presumes Pip to be married and 'little Pip' is his son, while Pip can only *assume* from her saddened look, touch and voice that she now has a heart to understand what his heart '*used* to be'. The 'poor dream' (p. 482) does seem to be finally over. Pip is still a childless bachelor and the suggestion is that Estella is childless too: this would be considered a sad fate indeed by the Victorian reader.

The revised additional Chapter 59 as we have it now is a much more orchestrated affair. Dickens wrote to his friend John Forster that he had 'put in as pretty a little piece of writing as I could, and I have no doubt the story will be more acceptable through the alteration'. Satis House and the Brewery have gone, but the garden is still there and the ivy symbolically striking new roots 'and growing green on low mounds of ruin' (p. 482) is suggestive of fresh hope. There is a greater sense of **closure** with these two meeting once more in the place where their fateful relationship began, and there may be some reassuring **symbolism** in the rising of the mist – or does it mean Pip's misapprehensions continue? The final sentence is deliberately ambiguous and Dickens changed it several times. The serial version and First Edition read 'I saw the shadow of no parting from her' (p. 484) but Dickens later altered this to 'I saw no shadow of another parting from her'. Both versions are enigmatic and clearly meant to be so. We read the story from Pip's point of view and Estella's thoughts and her story are hidden from us. She does say 'And will continue friends *apart*' (p. 484), but in the final sentence Dickens seems to collude, up to a point, with his hero's 'poor dream'.

CHECK THE BOOK

For more on Victorian serialisation see John Butt and Katherine Tillotson's classic *Dickens at Work* (1957).

LANGUAGE AND STYLE

A rereading of the opening chapter of *Great Expectations* demonstrates something of the extraordinary range and power of Dickens' language. After a brief statement about his self-naming, which is important in itself as it instigates the whole debate about identity in the novel, Pip goes on to entertain us with an amusing description of his family graves, their inscriptions, and what he, as a small boy, made of them. The older, sophisticated narrator explores the imaginative but essentially innocent mind of his younger self with a wit and vocabulary that is anything but childlike. Then this introduction into young Pip's growing awareness of 'the identity of things' (p. 3) is violently interrupted by the sound of a 'terrible voice' that demands 'wittles' and a file or promises that awful retribution will follow. Dramatic dialogue between the child and the convict follows. Much like Pip himself, the reader is suddenly thrown upside down into an elemental, nightmare world of mud, stones, frogs and eels, where being eaten alive is a real possibility and pirates come to life before returning to hook themselves back on to their gibbets.

This tension between an urbane, educated, retrospective narrative voice and other, more urgent forms of direct speech, is a feature of the book throughout. The dominant tone is that of Pip telling his story, but there are a great variety of other languages, different voices, and more eccentric styles within this dominant discourse.

 QUESTION

G. K. Chesterton praised the 'rush and energy' in Dickens' description of Trabb's Boy. He thought it something that 'no one else could do'. Discuss the comedy in *Great Expectations* and Dickens' treatment of the minor characters in the light of this comment.

This is not to suggest that Pip's own voice lacks range and variety. As we see, he can investigate his own childish terror vividly, but he can also recreate Pumblechook's nemesis with the tar-water to great comic effect. In delicious slow motion, Pumblechook's 'appalling spasmodic whooping-cough dance', his 'plunging and expectorating' is described from a child's point of view but with an educated adult's syntax and vocabulary (Chapter 4, p. 28). Later he can detail Trabb's boy's revenge against himself with the same leisurely attention to detail: 'With a shock he became aware of me, and was severely visited as before; but this time his motion was rotatory, and he staggered round and round me with knees more afflicted, and with uplifted hands as if beseeching for mercy' (Chapter 30, pp. 245–6). As narrator, Pip has a sharp way with **irony**, particularly when it is directed against his own pretensions. In Chapter 19 he goes to church with Joe 'and thought, perhaps, the clergyman wouldn't have read that about the rich man and the kingdom of Heaven, if he had known all' (pp. 146–7).

Despite the humour and the comic episodes, the prevailing tone of Pip's narration is one of resigned melancholy. Sometimes the reader feels like an eavesdropper listening to the mature Pip's reflections on his earlier self. The beginning of Chapter 29, when he reflects on his love for Estella, is a good example of this. We are persuaded that Pip is explaining the matter to himself as much as to us, his readers. At other times, like the final paragraph of Chapter 9, he addresses us more directly. Dickens is at pains to make us share Pip's trials and tribulations; he wishes to draw us into a relationship with him. Pip can be witty, even cruel, at others' expense as when he observes that Joe's education 'like Steam, was yet in its infancy' (Chapter 7, p. 46) but he can also show great empathy and poetic sensibility. In Chapter 38 he sees the active evidence of Miss Havisham's perverse, necrophiliac life in 'the falls of the cobwebs from the centre-piece, in the crawlings of the spiders on the cloth, in the tracks of the mice as they betook their little quickened hearts behind the panels, and in the gropings and pausings of the beetles on the floor' (p. 303).

So the style and language of Dickens' main narrator is indeed that of a gentleman; it is polished and urbane, well educated and well modulated. However, Pip is a willing reporter of those whose speech is anything but educated and refined. He captures the voices of a wide cross-section of society, stressing degrees of verbal formality, distinctive vocabularies and characteristic oddities of syntax. These range from Miss Havisham's self-dramatising formalities: 'So proud, so proud! So hard, so hard!' (Chapter 38, p. 305) to the pompous, self-educated aggrandisement of Pumblechook where the distinctive spelling stresses the tone and qualities of the speech: 'I forgit myself when I take such an interest in your breakfast, as to wish your frame, exhausted by the debilitating effects of prodigygality, to be stimulated by the 'olesome nourishment of your forefathers' (Chapter 58, p. 475).

One of Dickens' great achievements as a novelist is the respect he accords to the demotic energy of lower class speech. Chapter 42 is a good example. Magwitch opens his story, so similar to Pip's in some respects, so different in others, in a language that shows a feel for a balanced sentence and a vivid simile as well as using an irregular passive and a faulty past tense: 'I've been done everything to, pretty well – except hanged. I've been locked up, as much as a silver tea-kettle. I've been carted here and carted there, and put out of this town and put out of that town, and stuck in the stocks, and whipped and worried and drove' (p. 346).

'Whatsume'er the failings on his part, Remember reader he were that good in his hart' (Chapter 7, p. 47). We may not feel Joe's

CHECK THE BOOK
Harry Stone in *Dickens and the Invisible World* (1979) has some insightful comments in Chapter 8 on the symbolism of the jewels that Miss Havisham hangs in Estella's hair and how this relates to Estella's own hard, cold personality, as well as providing some contexts for the character of Miss Havisham herself.

QUESTION

Demonstrate how
Dickens' distinctive
use of language
expresses his
moral values and
his social criticism
in *Great
Expectations*.

'manifest pride' in his epitaph on his father, carried off in 'a purple leptic fit' (p. 47) is altogether justified and he cuts a poor or comic figure in hostile or unfamiliar surroundings. His language is inadequate to the complex demands of the world beyond the forge; like Jaggers we are sometimes encouraged to view him as 'the village idiot' (Chapter 18, p. 142). But at other times, his language has a defining moral purpose that finds clear rhythms and a simple clarity shaming the more elaborate, evasive speech of others: 'I'm awful dull, but I hope I've beat out something nigh the rights of this at last. And so GOD bless you, dear old Pip, old chap, GOD bless you!' (Chapter 27, p. 224).

Behind Pip lies Dickens, of course. Along with other of his texts, *Great Expectations* shows all the typical Dickensian tricks of style that emphasise his distinctive view of the world. In particular, there are several fine examples of the imaginative transference that makes people perform like robots but objects acquire a life and energy of their own. Pip's bed at the Hummums Hotel in Chapter 45 is 'a despotic monster … straddling over the whole place, putting one of his arbitrary legs into the fire-place and another into the doorway, and squeezing the wretched little washing-stand in quite a Divinely Righteous manner' (p. 366). On the other hand, when Pip first studies Wemmick, he sees him as made out of wood: 'I found him to be a dry man, rather short in stature, with a square wooden face, whose expression seemed to have been imperfectly chipped out with a dull-edged chisel' (Chapter 21, p. 171). When Pip gives Estella tea on her arrival in London , 'a meek little muffin' is 'confined with the utmost precaution under a strong iron cover' (Chapter 33, p. 268) but Pumblechook and Wemmick can behave mechanically; one keeps repeating 'May I? *May* I?' sycophantically, as he shakes Pip's hand in Chapter 19, the other's mouth changes shape as his arm steals round Miss Skiffins' waist (Chapter 37). Of course this can be very entertaining, but as a technique has its serious uses. It expresses Dickens' view of a society where material things are valued more than people and people are treated like objects.

IMAGERY AND SYMBOLISM

Great Expectations may be read like a poem, and careful attention
should be paid to Dickens' suggestive and associative uses of
language. Image clusters with **symbolic** resonances are particularly
concentrated in the opening chapters dealing with Pip's early
childhood. Events on the marsh and at Satis House that have such a
powerful impact on young Pip bring with them sets of images that
continue to haunt him, however high he rises in the social scale. The
marsh is a bleak landscape of crime, guilt and punishment that
becomes symbolic of a sense of original sin that Pip cannot shake
off. It is an elemental world of mud, water, mist and wind, where
the gibbet, image of retribution, dominates the low skyline.
Magwitch appears to erupt violently from the marsh and to be part
of it. 'Soaked in water and smothered in mud', he wishes he were 'a
frog. Or a eel' (Chapter 1, p. 6). He claims Pip as an accomplice and
the images of that bond, the stolen file and the leg-iron, will never
quite go away. It seems that Pip is, in Mr Hubble's terse phrase,
'Naterally wicious' (Chapter 4, p. 26).

When Magwitch is led in chains back to the black Hulk, a 'wicked
Noah's ark' (Chapter 5, p. 40), it appears to young Pip that the
prison ship is chained like the prisoners, and chains, fetters and
manacles of various kinds continue to dominate his young life. 'This
boy must be bound' (Chapter 13, p. 104) Pumblechook insists, and
on arrival at the Town Hall to sign his indentures, Pip is given a
tract with a wood-cut showing a young man 'fitted up with a
perfect sausage-shop of fetters' (p. 105). The marshes are, in the
local dialect, 'meshes' that entangle him and never lose their grip.
On his arrival in London, the marsh landscape of dirt, gibbet, crime
and punishment, reasserts itself in Little Britain and Barnard's Inn.
In Jaggers' office the death masks of two hanged criminals look
down on Pip from the wall, and he narrowly escapes execution
himself outside Herbert's lodgings when a rotten window comes
down 'like the guillotine' (Chapter 21, p. 174).

In Chapter 8, Pip finds himself in another landscape of coercion and
violence, but it appears to be of a different kind and is seductive as

CONTEXT

New South Wales
was no longer a
penal colony when
Dickens came to
write *Great
Expectations*.
Transportation
there was finally
abolished in 1851
although
discontinued
earlier. Magwitch's
success story,
though rare, was
not impossible.
The death penalty
for returned
'Transports' was
revoked in 1835
but not enforced
after 1810.

CHECK THE BOOK

In her book on *Great Expectations,* Anny Sadrin has a detailed chapter on the dating of the novel.

well as terrifying. Satis House is a fairy-tale world of arrested time and morbid decay where Miss Havisham plays out her theatrical psychodrama of bitterness and grief. The disused brewery, the rotting barrels, the overgrown garden, the empty dove-cote, are resonant images of life denied, but they have a fascination for the blacksmith's boy that finds expression in his fanciful reinterpretation of events for the credulous folk at the forge (Chapter 9).

But the world of the marsh and Satis House are not as far apart as they seem. The dirt and decay of Miss Havisham's chamber are associated with the elemental mud of the village graveyard. When Pip first sees Miss Havisham, he remembers being taken to see 'a skeleton in the ashes of a rich dress, that had been dug out of a vault' (Chapter 8, p. 58). The mist on the marshes and the spiders' webs on the hedges as Pip goes to visit his convict in Chapter 3 are recalled by the smoke from the fire and the cobwebs on the cake in Chapter 11. Pip's vision of a hanging Miss Havisham from a beam in the brewery seems transposed from the image of the hanging pirate in Chapter 1, and the cold wind of the marshes blows through the disused brewery too. Through such powers of suggestion, Dickens reveals the links between crime and social oppression. There is a bond between the outcast and the exploited child. The plot connections between Newgate and Satis House are already anticipated in the imagery that Dickens uses.

Dickens is very bold in his use of symbolism. We only get the most cursory explanation for Miss Havisham's grief or the reasons for her actions. Instead of examining Miss Havisham's psychology in an ordered, rational way, he allows the rotting bride cake to act as a visible expression of her embittered, self-destructive psyche. Its 'black fungus' (Chapter 11, p. 84) is a visible extension of herself, as she seems to understand, when she invites her parasitic relations to feast on her like the speckled spiders and the black beetles when she is laid on the great dining table after her death.

Other examples of the use of material objects as visible extensions of inner feelings include Mrs Joe's 'square impregnable bib' (Chapter 2, p. 8) full of pins and needles which expresses her resentful lack of maternal feeling and, later in the novel, Wemmick's

IMAGERY AND SYMBOLISM

castle reveals his determination to protect his private life from the demands of the outside world. Estella is associated with stars and Miss Havisham's jewels. She is bright, but cold and remote.

Certain key images or repeated events weave their way through the text, gathering meaning and significance as they appear. For example, characters are judged by the way they feed themselves and each other. Pip sympathises with the convict on the marshes when he eats like a ravenous dog in Chapter 3, but not on his return in Chapter 39. Estella treats Pip like 'a dog in disgrace' (p. 62) when she brings him his meal in Chapter 8, but Herbert educates him in gentlemanly table manners with tactful forbearance in Chapter 22. Perverted Miss Havisham seems to anticipate being eaten with more relish than eating. Jaggers tells Pip he never will see Miss Havisham eat: 'She wanders around in the night, and then she lays hands on such food as she takes' (Chapter 29, p. 241).

Hand imagery plays a crucial role in defining the nature of human bonds and commitments. Jaggers constantly washes his hands as if to deny human contact. Wemmick is surprised when Pip first offers his hand in London, but will shake that of a condemned criminal before he goes to the gallows (Chapter 32). Pumblechook shakes the hands of the newly affluent Pip with sycophantic persistence in Chapter 19 but exhibits 'the same fat five fingers' with 'ostentatious clemency' (p. 475) when he returns to the town penniless in Chapter 58. Pip magnanimously offers to shake Joe's grimy work-stained hand as he departs after his sister's funeral (Chapter 35), but shrinks away when Magwitch returns 'holding out both his hands' (Chapter 39, p. 314). Finally, however, he learns to hold the dying convict's hand in selfless love (Chapter 56).

It is possible to see many such patterns in this novel and read significance into them. Other repeated images include those of fire, clothes and animals. Dickens' language is rich and suggestive. One should be careful, however, not to lean too heavily on one set of images at the expense of others, and to try to make one's reading of the text as generous and inclusive as possible.

? QUESTION

Discuss the significance of food and eating in *Great Expectations*.

PART FOUR

CRITICAL HISTORY

 CHECK THE BOOK

Edited selections of some of the early reviews of the novel can be found in Tredall's *Reader's Guide*. For a fuller, more detailed documentation of Dickens's early reception and growing reputation, readers should consult *Dickens: The Critical Heritage*, (1971), edited by Philip Collins.

THE GROTESQUE TRAGI-COMIC CONCEPTION

In October 1860, Dickens wrote to Forster on the progress of his new novel stressing the humour of the opening chapters: 'I have put a child and a good-natured foolish man, in relations that seem to me very funny.' He also mentioned that he had got in 'the pivot on which the story will turn'. This was 'the grotesque tragi-comic conception that first encouraged me'.

The idea of a convict funding a gentleman was clearly the initial inspiration behind the novel, but Dickens was at pains to stress the humour and comedy in the situation. He had been made aware that his readers had felt the lack of comedy in his novels since the publication of *David Copperfield* in 1850. This novel was to be an attempt to return to his early manner as a humorist. In this he was only partially successful. The early reviews were mixed for, in general, Dickens' contemporaries preferred the early, exuberant comic fictions to the later novels that contained a comprehensive critique of their society. Some reviewers saw Dickens' efforts as a return to the old manner, others felt that his powers were weakening. Still, Dickens succeeded in his primary objective; circulation of *All the Year Round* picked up and the sales of the novel in volume form were good.

LATER CRITICAL HISTORY

Like many Victorian writers, Dickens' reputation waned in the earlier years of the twentieth century. Although he never lacked popularity among general readers, many artists and intellectuals reacted against his perceived sentimentality and undisciplined excess as a novelist. This changed rapidly in the 1940s and 1950s when some important reappraisals of his work were written. The later novels were now particularly favoured, and *Great Expectations* was seen as one of the greatest, if not the best. This view of the novel has not changed. It is still seen as one of the most powerfully conceived and highly organised of all his works.

Influential general essays from this period that are often anthologised and still well worth reading include those by Edmund Wilson, George Orwell and Dorothy Van Ghent. Wilson's essay, 'Dickens: the two Scrooges' (see **Further reading** for all the following title references), was a pioneering attempt to psychologise Dickens, stressing the traumatic effect of the blacking factory episode. Orwell's most lucid and readable assessment, 'Charles Dickens', emphasises his morality, while Van Ghent's essay, 'The Dickens World: a view from Todgers's', explores the nature of his imagination and the suggestive power of his imagery and **symbolism**. Her reading of *Great Expectations* is particularly interesting. So, too, are Humphry House's views on the novel in his book, *The Dickens World*. This was a witty but scholarly attempt to place Dickens in the context of his time.

Important articles and books with chapters on the novel continued the debate over the next twenty years and show the variety of criticism that is possible. For example, Julian Moynahan's essay, 'The Hero's Guilt: the Case of *Great Expectations*', is a provoking analysis of Orlick's role in the novel, but approaches like his are refuted by Q. D. Leavis in her combative essay, 'How we must read *Great Expectations*'. Her emphasis is on historical context and sociological detail, but in his book, *Dickens and the Invisible World: Fairy Tales, Fantasy and Novel-Making,* Harry Stone examines the 'other worldly' fantastic element in the novel, as well as some of the likely sources for Miss Havisham.

CHECK THE BOOK
See Dorothy Van Ghent's essay on Dickens in *The English Novel: Form and Function* (1961) for a lively discussion on Dickens' imagery.

SOME CONTEMPORARY APPROACHES

HISTORICAL APPROACHES

In a compressed and tightly argued article in 1954, G. Robert Stange saw the novel as part of a great European tradition of education novels, 'a moral fable' and 'the classic legend of the nineteenth century' (see **Further reading**). Scholars are still working to fill in the full historical context for this novel and so retrieve meanings that may have been obvious to Dickens' first readers, but can get quickly lost to subsequent generations. Robin Gilmour's book, *The Idea of the Gentleman in the Victorian Novel*, (see **Further reading**), has an excellent chapter on *Great Expectations* that follows the tradition of Humphry House and Q. D. Leavis.

STRUCTURALIST APPROACHES

Structuralism takes many forms, but the emphasis is on the material from which the novel is made, rather than its content. For example, such an approach might concentrate on the plots in which Pip finds himself and the narrative strategies that Dickens uses. Rather than concentrate on Pip as a coherent 'character', the emphasis would be on how he, and others, are constructed for specific purposes from traditional literary roles. Dickens does not create from scratch; he has to use the available literary material at hand. Anny Sadrin has an interesting chapter in her book on *Great Expectations* (see **Further reading**) which analyses the hybrid nature of Dickens' narrative, showing how it overlays a realistic plot with a romantic one to great ironic effect.

PSYCHOLOGICAL APPROACHES

CHECK THE FILM

In David Lean's film, Joe and Biddy see Pip off on the coach, so considerably softening Dickens' criticism of Pip's behaviour.

Great Expectations has always been a favourite text for psychological analysis. Pip needs a father and mother, and is the victim of several surrogate parents. His love for Estella is obsessive and self-destructive. Not for nothing does *Hamlet*, however comically, feature in this novel. The substance of the novel may be seen as Pip's search for an identity through a lost father figure, and eventual acceptance of his lowly, unhappy origins. Peter Brooks' essay, 'Repetition, Repression and Return: *Great Expectations* and the Study of Plot' (see **Further reading**) examines the way in which the structure of the novel is symptomatic of Pip's repression. He shows that Pip must be 'cured' of plots. Brooks uses Freudian models for his analysis of the plot, but Steven Connor uses the theories of the French psychoanalyst Jacques Lacan to discuss how Pip is caught up and forced to play out the disturbed desires of others although he feels these desires to be his own (see **Further reading**).

FEMINIST AND GENDER APPROACHES

Feminists would not see Pip's version of events as neutral or unbiased but a product of a male point of view. They would examine this text in the light of Victorian attitudes to women, and Dickens' in particular. They might see Dickens' treatment of Mrs Joe, Estella and Miss Havisham as evidence of his own troubled relationships with women and repressed hostility towards them. Lucy Frost discusses this in her article 'Taming to Improve: Dickens and the Women in *Great Expectations*'. In her article '"If He Should Turn and Beat Her": Violence, Desire, and the Woman's Story in *Great Expectations*' Hilary Schor reads the text 'against the grain' to make us see the story from Estella's point of view (see **Further reading**). Claire Tomalin has filled in an important missing context to the later fiction in her study of Dickens' relationship with his mistress, Ellen Ternan, which feminists have found useful in their efforts to revise traditional readings of his novels. Gender readings are interested to show how sexual identity, bonding and desire are inscribed in the language of texts. William Cohen's 'Manual Conduct in *Great Expectations*' is a witty example of this kind of criticism. He focuses on the 'hand' imagery in the novel but with a very different emphasis from more traditional readings (see **Further reading**).

CHECK THE BOOK

See John Carey's *The Violent Effigy: a Study of Dickens' Imagination* (1973) for a discussion on Dickens' linking of violence with sexuality.

PART FIVE

BACKGROUND

CHARLES DICKENS

Dickens was born in 1812, the son of a clerk in the Naval Pay Office. His early childhood was spent in Portsmouth and then Chatham, near the Thames marshes where *Great Expectations* is set, before the family moved to London when he was nine. In 1824, Dickens' father got into severe financial difficulties and was imprisoned in the Marshalsea Prison for debt. For four months Dickens worked in Warren's blacking warehouse near the Thames until the family's fortunes improved. This was a humiliating experience for him; he never forgot it, and kept it a close secret from all save John Forster, his first biographer and most intimate friend. The sense of abandonment and sudden awareness of the fragility of class distinctions was to haunt him for the rest of his life.

In 1827, Dickens went to work in a law firm and later turned to journalism. Sketches for newspapers and journals led to the publication of *The Pickwick Papers* in 1836–7 which was an immediate success. At the age of twenty-four, Dickens became a celebrity and never lost his position as a major Victorian public figure and man of letters. Public success concealed a troubled private life, however. The early courtship of Maria Beadnell, a banker's daughter, came to nothing and marriage to Catherine Hogarth in 1836 brought him many children but much frustration and unhappiness.

In 1856, he bought Gad's Hill, considered to be the original for Satis House, a large mansion on the outskirts of Rochester that he had admired as a small boy. Two years later he separated from his wife and soon this became his permanent home. Despite his success and many profitable activities that included editing his own journals, *Household Words* and *All the Year Round*, as well as the popular public readings from his own works, Dickens was never free of financial anxiety. His later years were also complicated by his clandestine relationship with a young actress, Ellen Ternan. He died in 1870, aged fifty-nine, from exhaustion and overwork.

> **CONTEXT**
>
> Dickens' own prolonged and unsuccessful courtship of Maria Beadnell (1830–33) may be the source for Pip's unhappy infatuation with Estella. Also, at the time of writing this novel, Dickens was conducting a clandestine affair with a much younger woman, the actress Ellen Ternan.

HIS OTHER WORKS

Dickens was a prolific writer, sometimes beginning a new novel while still finishing the current one. He completed fourteen novels in all, interspersed with many other literary, business and philanthropic activities. *Great Expectations* is one of the darker, more reflective novels of his later years but much more intimate than the panoramic, social novels of the 1850s like *Bleak House* (1853) and *Little Dorrit* (1857). He was constantly experimenting and innovating in his fiction right up to his death; the private, introspective tone of this novel is in marked contrast to *The Tale of Two Cities*, the historical novel on the French Revolution that immediately preceded it and also published in *All the Year Round*.

It is useful to compare *Great Expectations* with two earlier novels, *Oliver Twist* (1838) and *David Copperfield* (1850). Although containing passages of grim realism on the workhouse and criminal London, the former uses a fairy-tale plot that Dickens treats ironically in *Great Expectations*. Oliver is a foundling but really of genteel birth. He is a passive, silent figure, often absent from the plot, who is restored to his rightful inheritance by the efforts of others. This, of course, is the exact opposite of Pip's story. He is the most lowly of Dickens' heroes; he thinks he has a magical helper who will make him a gentleman, but has to learn he is the son of a poor man after all.

David Copperfield is also of interest to readers of *Great Expectations* because it represents Dickens' first attempt to write a fictional autobiography in the first person; indeed Dickens reread it before commencing his new novel. Dickens explores the traumatic episode in the blacking warehouse much more directly in this book but David is more secure in his middle-class status than his author ever was. He is a gentleman's son who is rescued by a kindly relative and restored to his natural position in society. David's narration is leisurely and expansive, much like Dickens' own authorial one in other novels. *Great Expectations* represents more of a challenge because Dickens has to find a first person voice that is more distinct from his own. It is generally agreed that in this novel Dickens explores his mixed feelings about his past much more rigorously

CHECK THE BOOK

Claire Tomalin gives an interesting account of the 'secret history' of Dickens' life with Ellen Ternan in *The Invisible Woman: The Story of Ellen Ternan and Charles Dickens* (1991).

CHECK THE NET

There is more about Australian penal colonies under 'Prisons, Crime and the Law' at: **http://www.umd.umich.edu/casl/hum/eng/classes/434/geweb/**

than in the earlier one, although the actual events are entirely fictional.

HISTORICAL BACKGROUND

Great Expectations is set in the early years of the nineteenth century, just before the Victorian period. It is possible to date the main action of the novel around the years 1807–23. This means that there is a significant gap between the time of publication and the setting of the novel itself. Dickens' first readers would be looking back to a cruder, less civilised time and be able to measure the progress that society had made during their own lives. The Hulks, transportation and hanging for minor offences belong to an older, brutal penal system that had been reformed. Pip is representative of an emergent middle class that had grown up with the new century. Many of the contemporary readers of this novel would see in Pip's story a version of their own life history and trace the beginnings of a more complicated society. Joe's life at the forge might have a nostalgic appeal, but it belonged to the irretrievable past. The definition of a gentleman had also changed. To be one was now an aspiration that all educated, hard-working men could aspire to.

LITERARY BACKGROUND

Great Expectations is a fine example of an education novel or **bildungsroman**, a form of fiction that came into prominence in the nineteenth century. Other examples include Charlotte Brontë's *Jane Eyre*, George Eliot's *Mill on the Floss* and Thomas Hardy's *Jude the Obscure*. These novels focus on an unaccommodated child, often an orphan, who has to grow up and find a place in a hostile world. These novels invariably contain an autobiographical element, but the form is also used to explore the complications and corruptions of society. Many of these novels are set a little way back in the recent past in order to explore social issues with greater security and confidence. The movement of the hero or heroine away from their roots in provincial society to a more sophisticated life in the city is also a common feature.

Great Expectations also shows the traces of an older form of fiction called the **picaresque novel**. The term comes from the word 'picar' meaning 'rogue', and the best example of such a fiction in English is *Tom Jones* (1749) by the eighteenth-century novelist, Henry Fielding. Such novels tell of the adventures and misadventures of low-life characters, often foundlings, as they travel through life and encounter different sections of society. Prophesies of a bad end are narrowly averted and the character is eventually accepted into society.

Another, more immediate influence is the 'sensation' novel popularised by Wilkie Collins, a friend and literary rival of Dickens. *A Woman in White* preceded *Great Expectations* in *All the Year Round* and was very popular. It set a fashion for novels with mystery plots, detection, suspense and violent action, all of which feature in this novel.

CHECK THE BOOK

For issues concerning the Empire and its consequences for literature including *Great Expectations*, see Edward Said's *Culture and Imperialism* (1993). Robert Hughes gives the background to the use of Australia as a penal colony in *The Fatal Shore* (1987), and in *Jack Maggs* (1997) the Australian novelist Peter Carey rewrites a version of the Magwitch story, drawing it in from the margins into a more central position.

History	Author's life	Literature
1788 First convict settlement is founded in Australia		
		1789 Jeremy Bentham, *Introduction to Principles of Morals and Legislation*
1802 First Act of Parliament is passed protecting factory workers		
		1811 Jane Austen, *Sense and Sensibility*
	1812 Born	
	1812-19 Spends early childhood in Portsmouth then Chatham	**1813** Jane Austen, *Pride and Prejudice*
		1815 Lord Byron, *Collected Works*
1819 First Factory Act is passed to restrict employment of children in mines	**1819** Moves to London with parents	
		1820 Thomas Malthus, *Principles of Political Economy*
	1824 Dickens' father is imprisoned for debt; Dickens works in Warren's blacking warehouse until family's fortunes improve	
1825 First passenger railway opens		
	1827 Starts work in a law firm	
		1830 William Cobbett, *Rural Rides*
1832 Cholera epidemic sweeps across England. The Great Reform Bill is passed. Last gibbeting	**1832** Becomes a journalist	
1834 Parish workhouses introduced. 'Tolpuddle Martyrs' are convicted and transported to Australia. Returning illegally from transportation ceased to be punishable by death		
	1836 Marries Catherine Hogarth. *Pickwick Papers*	
1837 Victoria becomes Queen. 'Hulks' system condemned		
	1838 *Oliver Twist*	

History	Author's life	Literature
1840 Transportation to New South Wales abolished	**1840-41** *The Old Curiosity Shop*	
1842 Employment in mines of women and children under ten is outlawed		**1842** Edwin Chadwick, *Inquiry into the Sanatory Condition of the Labouring Population*
	1843 *A Christmas Carol*	
		1845 Benjamin Disraeli, *Sybil*
		1847 Charlotte Bronte, *Jane Eyre*. Karl Marx and Frederick Engels, *The Communist Manifesto*
1848 Municipalities are empowered to set up local boards of health. Widespread civil unrest sweeps across Europe		
	1850 *David Copperfield*	
1851 Great Exhibition in London		
	1853 *Bleak House*	
	1854 *Hard Times*	
	1856 Buys Gad's Hill near Rochester	
	1857 *Little Dorrit*	
1858 Last 'Hulk' closed	**1858** Separates from Catherine	
		1859 Charles Darwin, *Origin of the Species*. Samuel Smiles, *Self-Help*
	1860-61 *Great Expectations*	**1860** George Eliot, *The Mill on the Floss*. Wilkie Collins, *The Woman in White*
		1861 George Eliot, *Silas Marner*
		1863 John Stuart Mill, *Utilitarianism*
	1864-65 *Our Mutual Friend*	
1867 Some sections of the working class are given the vote for the first time		**1867** Karl Marx, *Das Kapital*
1869 Imprisonment for debt is abolished		
1870 Forster's Elementary Education Act establishes School Boards with power to set up schools in areas where there are no church schools	**1870** Dies of overwork and exhaustion. *Edwin Drood* left unfinished at his death	

FURTHER READING

Peter Ackroyd, *Dickens*, Sinclair-Stevenson, London, 1990
A lively and readable modern biography

Peter Brooks, *Reading for the Plot: Design and Intention in Narrative*, Oxford University Press, 1984
This contains his essay on *Great Expectations* 'Repetition, Repression and Return: *Great Expectations* and the Study of Plot', mentioned above

John Carey, *The Violent Effigy: A Study of Dickens' Imagination*, Faber, London, 1973
A stimulating general discussion of Dickens' bizarre imagery and fixations that includes comments on *Great Expectations*

Janice Carlisle (ed.), *Charles Dickens: 'Great Expectations'*, Bedford Books, Barton,1996
This is a volume in the Case Studies in Contemporary Criticism series that has the text and five modern critical perspectives. Included here are Hilary Schor's feminist essay, '"If He Should Turn to and Beat Her": Violence, Desire and the Woman's Story in *Great Expectations*', and selections from a highly provocative and original essay by William Cohen, 'Manual Conduct in *Great Expectations*', that explores the suggestive language of homoeroticism in the text

Philip Collins, *Dickens: The Critical Heritage*, Routledge, London, 1987

Steven Connor, *Charles Dickens*, Blackwell, Oxford, 1985
This contains a demanding but rewarding chapter on the novel using sophisticated concepts from Lacanian psychology

Robert Garis, *The Dickens Theatre: A Reassessment of the Novels*, Clarendon Press, Oxford, 1965
Emphasises the theatrical and deliberately artificial aspects of Dickens' art

Robin Gilmour, *The Idea of the Gentleman in the Victorian Novel*, Routledge, London, 1981
There is a long chapter on the novel

Barbara Hardy, *The Moral Art of Dickens: Essays*, Athlone Press, London, 1970

Humphry House, *The Dickens World*, Oxford University Press, 1941

Edgar Johnson, *Charles Dickens: His Tragedy and Triumph*, Gollancz, London, 1953, Revised and abridged, 1977
A conventional academic biography

F. R. and Q. D Leavis., *Dickens the Novelist*, Chatto & Windus, London, 1970
This includes the essay 'How we must read *Great Expectations*' mentioned above

J. Hillis Miller, *Charles Dickens: The World of his Novels*, Harvard University Press, 1958

George Orwell, *Inside the Whale*, Secker and Warburg, London, 1940
  This includes his essay, 'Charles Dickens', which can also be found in *The Collected Essays, Journalism and Letters of George Orwell*, Volume 1, Secker and Warburg, 1968

Norman Page, (ed.), *Hard Times, Great Expectations and Our Mutual Friend*, Macmillan Casebook, 1979
  Julian Moynahan's essay, 'The Hero's Guilt: the Case of *Great Expectations*', can be found most easily here

Anny Sadrin, *Great Expectations*, Unwin Hyman, London, 1988
  A very useful volume in the Unwin Critical Library series

Paul Schlike, *Oxford Reader's Companion to Dickens*, Oxford University Press, 1999
  A good general reference guide

Roger D. Sell, (ed.), *Great Expectations*, Macmillan New Casebook Series, Basingstoke, 1994
  This has a wide selection of contemporary critical essays, including extracts from Brooks, Gilmour and Sadrin mentioned above. Lucy's Frost article, 'Taming to Improve: Dickens and the Women in *Great Expectations*' can also be found here. This volume also contains a useful bibliography

Harry Stone, *Dickens and the Invisible World: Fairy Tales, Fantasy and Novel Making*, Indiana University Press, USA, 1979
  This argues for a more fabulist and magical view of the text in the two long chapters that end the book

Jeremy Tambling, *Dickens, Violence and the Modern State: Dreams of the Scaffold*, Macmillan, Basingstoke, 1995
  Using ideas drawn from the influential post-structuralist philosopher Michel Foucault, a chapter on the novel demonstrates the way in which institutions discipline and control Dickens' society

Clare Tomalin, *The Invisible Woman: The Story of Nelly Ternan and Charles Dickens*, Penguin, London, 1991

Nicolas Tredell, (ed.), *Charles Dickens: Great Expectations*, *A Reader's Guide to Essential Criticism*, Icon Books, Cambridge, 2000
  A valuable anthology of criticism linked by a thoughtful and instructive commentary, this includes selections of material not easily obtainable elsewhere like extracts from the early reviews, Robert G. Stang's seminal discussion, 'Expectations Well Lost; Dickens' Fable for His Time', *College English*, 16, (October, 1954), pp. 9-17, and more recent feminist and gender criticism like the Cohen article mentioned above and Catherine Waters' book, *Dickens and the Politics of the Family*, Cambridge University Press, 1997. Tredell traces the growth of Dickens' reputation and assesses the contributions made by various critical schools over the decades in a concise and readable way

FURTHER READING

Dorothy Van Ghent, *The English Novel: Form and Function*, Holt, Rinehart and Winston, New York, 1953

Her important essay, 'The Dickens World: a view from Todgers's', on Dickens' symbolism, can be found here

Edmund Wilson, *The Wound and the Bow*, W.H. Allen & Co, London, 1941

His essay on Dickens, 'Dickens: the two Scrooges', was republished in this volume

LITERARY TERMS

bildungsroman a novel concerning the education and development of the main character

caricature to get at the essence of an idea or personality by significant, selective exaggeration

closure the impression of completion at the end of a literary work

fable a narrative designed to illustrate a moral truth

farce, farcical a form of drama or acting with exaggerated comic action

gothic in eighteenth- or nineteenth-century literature, an imaginative projection of extreme and alarming experience

idyll an idealised portrayal of happy innocence, usually in a country setting

irony, ironic using words in a sense or context that implies the opposite meaning to what is actually said

melodramatic exaggerated expression of simple emotions

metaphor, metaphoric using language to identify one thing in terms of another

metonymy, metonymic the substitution of an attribute of something for the thing itself

mock-heroic writing in a comically exaggerated, solemn manner

motif a significantly repeated image or phrase

parody a mocking copy of something serious

pathos evoking pity or sadness

persona a mask used to project the writer's personality through another character

personification giving human qualities to inanimate objects

picaresque novel a favourite form of fiction in the eighteenth century, narrating the adventures of a rogue through all levels of society

parody a mocking copy

pun two meanings are drawn from a single word

satire, satirical holding up vice or folly to ridicule

simile describing one thing in terms of another by making the point of comparison obvious

symbol, symbolic investing objects in the material world with the suggestive power of abstract, complex ideas

AUTHOR OF THESE NOTES

Nigel Messenger has co-edited a volume of minor Victorian poetry and written on Joseph Conrad, E. M. Forster and D. H. Lawrence. He is a Senior Lecturer in the School of Arts and Humanities at Oxford Brookes University, where he lectures on Victorian and early Modern literature. He is author of the York Notes Advanced on E. M. Forster's *A Passage to India*.

General editors

Martin Gray, former Head of the Department of English Studies at the University of Stirling, and of Literary Studies at the University of Luton

Professor A. N. Jeffares, Emeritus Professor of English, University of Stirling

NOTES

Maya Angelou
I Know Why the Caged Bird Sings

Jane Austen
Pride and Prejudice

Alan Ayckbourn
Absent Friends

Elizabeth Barrett Browning
Selected Poems

Robert Bolt
A Man for All Seasons

Harold Brighouse
Hobson's Choice

Charlotte Brontë
Jane Eyre

Emily Brontë
Wuthering Heights

Shelagh Delaney
A Taste of Honey

Charles Dickens
David Copperfield
Great Expectations
Hard Times
Oliver Twist

Roddy Doyle
Paddy Clarke Ha Ha Ha

George Eliot
Silas Marner
The Mill on the Floss

Anne Frank
The Diary of a Young Girl

William Golding
Lord of the Flies

Oliver Goldsmith
She Stoops to Conquer

Willis Hall
The Long and the Short and the Tall

Thomas Hardy
Far from the Madding Crowd
The Mayor of Casterbridge
Tess of the d'Urbervilles
The Withered Arm and other Wessex Tales

L.P. Hartley
The Go-Between

Seamus Heaney
Selected Poems

Susan Hill
I'm the King of the Castle

Barry Hines
A Kestrel for a Knave

Louise Lawrence
Children of the Dust

Harper Lee
To Kill a Mockingbird

Laurie Lee
Cider with Rosie

Arthur Miller
The Crucible
A View from the Bridge

Robert O'Brien
Z for Zachariah

Frank O'Connor
My Oedipus Complex and Other Stories

George Orwell
Animal Farm

J.B. Priestley
An Inspector Calls
When We Are Married

Willy Russell
Educating Rita
Our Day Out

J.D. Salinger
The Catcher in the Rye

William Shakespeare
Henry IV Part I
Henry V
Julius Caesar
Macbeth
The Merchant of Venice
A Midsummer Night's Dream
Much Ado About Nothing

Romeo and Juliet
The Tempest
Twelfth Night

George Bernard Shaw
Pygmalion

Mary Shelley
Frankenstein

R.C. Sherriff
Journey's End

Rukshana Smith
Salt on the snow

John Steinbeck
Of Mice and Men

Robert Louis Stevenson
Dr Jekyll and Mr Hyde

Jonathan Swift
Gulliver's Travels

Robert Swindells
Daz 4 Zoe

Mildred D. Taylor
Roll of Thunder, Hear My Cry

Mark Twain
Huckleberry Finn

James Watson
Talking in Whispers

Edith Wharton
Ethan Frome

William Wordsworth
Selected Poems

A Choice of Poets

Mystery Stories of the Nineteenth Century including The Signalman

Nineteenth Century Short Stories

Poetry of the First World War

Six Women Poets

For the AQA Anthology:
Duffy & Armitage & Pre-1914 Poetry

Heaney & Clarke & Pre-1914 Poetry

Poems from Different Cultures

Margaret Atwood
Cat's Eye
The Handmaid's Tale

Jane Austen
Emma
Mansfield Park
Persuasion
Pride and Prejudice
Sense and Sensibility

Alan Bennett
Talking Heads

William Blake
*Songs of Innocence and of
Experience*

Charlotte Brontë
Jane Eyre
Villette

Emily Brontë
Wuthering Heights

Angela Carter
Nights at the Circus

Geoffrey Chaucer
The Franklin's Prologue and Tale
*The Merchant's Prologue and
Tale*
The Miller's Prologue and Tale
*The Prologue to the Canterbury
Tales*
*The Wife of Bath's Prologue and
Tale*

Samuel Coleridge
Selected Poems

Joseph Conrad
Heart of Darkness

Daniel Defoe
Moll Flanders

Charles Dickens
Bleak House
Great Expectations
Hard Times

Emily Dickinson
Selected Poems

John Donne
Selected Poems

Carol Ann Duffy
Selected Poems

George Eliot
Middlemarch
The Mill on the Floss

T.S. Eliot
Selected Poems
The Waste Land

F. Scott Fitzgerald
The Great Gatsby

E.M. Forster
A Passage to India

Brian Friel
Translations

Thomas Hardy
Jude the Obscure
The Mayor of Casterbridge
The Return of the Native
Selected Poems
Tess of the d'Urbervilles

Seamus Heaney
*Selected Poems from 'Opened
Ground'*

Nathaniel Hawthorne
The Scarlet Letter

Homer
The Iliad
The Odyssey

Aldous Huxley
Brave New World

Kazuo Ishiguro
The Remains of the Day

Ben Jonson
The Alchemist

James Joyce
Dubliners

John Keats
Selected Poems

Philip Larkin
*The Whitsun Weddings and
Selected Poems*

Christopher Marlowe
Doctor Faustus
Edward II

Arthur Miller
Death of a Salesman

John Milton
Paradise Lost Books I & II

Toni Morrison
Beloved

George Orwell
Nineteen Eighty-Four

Sylvia Plath
Selected Poems

Alexander Pope
*Rape of the Lock & Selected
Poems*

William Shakespeare
Antony and Cleopatra
As You Like It
Hamlet
Henry IV Part I
King Lear
Macbeth
Measure for Measure
The Merchant of Venice
A Midsummer Night's Dream
Much Ado About Nothing
Othello
Richard II
Richard III
Romeo and Juliet
The Taming of the Shrew
The Tempest
Twelfth Night
The Winter's Tale

George Bernard Shaw
Saint Joan

Mary Shelley
Frankenstein

Jonathan Swift
*Gulliver's Travels and A Modest
Proposal*

Alfred Tennyson
Selected Poems

Virgil
The Aeneid

Alice Walker
The Color Purple

Oscar Wilde
*The Importance of Being
Earnest*

Tennessee Williams
A Streetcar Named Desire
The Glass Menagerie

Jeanette Winterson
*Oranges Are Not the Only
Fruit*

John Webster
The Duchess of Malfi

Virginia Woolf
To the Lighthouse

William Wordsworth
*The Prelude and Selected
Poems*

W.B. Yeats
Selected Poems

Metaphysical Poets